# RUNNING
# FOR
# OUR
# LIVES

# RUNNING FOR OUR LIVES

Stories of ordinary
runners overcoming
extraordinary adversity

## RACHEL ANN CULLEN

Vertebrate Publishing, Sheffield
www.adventurebooks.com

# RUNNING
# FOR
# OUR
# LIVES

## RACHEL ANN CULLEN

First published in 2022 by Vertebrate Publishing.

Vertebrate Publishing
Omega Court, 352 Cemetery Road, Sheffield S11 8FT, United Kingdom.
www.adventurebooks.com

This book is a work of non-fiction. The author has stated to the publishers that, except in such minor respects not affecting the substantial accuracy of the work, the contents of the book are true. Some names and incidental details have been changed to protect the privacy of contributors.

A CIP catalogue record for this book is available from the British Library.

ISBN: 978-1-83981-139-5 (Paperback)
ISBN: 978-1-83981-140-1 (Ebook)
ISBN: 978-1-83981-141-8 (Audiobook)

10 9 8 7 6 5 4 3 2 1

Design by Jane Beagley, Vertebrate Publishing.
Production by Rosie Edwards, Vertebrate Publishing.
www.adventurebooks.com

Vertebrate Publishing is committed to printing on paper from sustainable sources.

MIX
Paper from responsible sources
FSC® C013056

Printed and bound in the UK by TJ Books Limited, Padstow, Cornwall.

*This book is dedicated to the memory of Ashling Murphy.*
*She was just going for a run.*

# CONTENTS

# PROLOGUE

**Diary entry, April 2015**

The doubtful voices come. Usually, it happens when I am trying my best to be brave, and I'm trying very hard to do that today. You see, I have an idea … and it won't go away. As I lie in the bath contemplating all that running has been in my life up to this point, my head keeps jumping between memories that are scorched into my brain. First, I am an overweight teen struggling to jog for more than a few minutes on a treadmill … then SWITCH … I am a thirty-seven-year-old woman winning a twenty-mile road race … SWITCH AGAIN … I am sixteen years old and struggling to breathe while barely even jogging up the slightest of inclines … SWITCH BACK AGAIN … I am crossing the finishing line of the London Marathon in three hours and seventeen minutes. As my head flips between the juxtaposed realities I have lived, I know that I want to share my story.

*'You can't do that!'* … *'Nobody even cares.'* … *'Why would they want to read your story?'* … *'Who do you think you are, Rachel?'* … *'Get back in your box.'*

When it happens, my first instinct is to scurry away and hide. *'It's a fair point,'* my logical mind responds to the mocking taunts. *'Why* should *anyone care? What do you have to say that anybody would possibly want to listen to? What's so special about your story? In fact, what's so special about you?'*

I am obedient by nature. My first instinct is to obey. WHAT AM I THINKING? For a brief moment it works, and I turn on my heels as though I'm about to do it – to head straight back into my box.

But then it happens. The tiniest fluttering of objection. And it is only

RUNNING FOR OUR LIVES

a fluttering, but I notice it and I am willing it to become stronger. I try to give it some space – room to expand as though it needs a quiet place and a growbag. My logical, over-thinking, self-berating mind is momentarily silenced. He is left huffing in frustrated breaths over in the corner. *'Why won't she LISTEN to me?'* he humphs, as I stand with my back to him, waiting for the brave voice to emerge.

I desperately want bravery to win. I don't want to be beaten back by self-doubt. I've long since realised that courage is not an end destination – it's a lifelong journey. Taking tiny steps forward. Clambering over self-doubt, dodging him when he stands in the way and shoving him out of the path when necessary. There isn't a moment when bravery holds up a victory salute or self-doubt reluctantly waves the white flag. He will always try to bully his way to the front – his bombast and arrogance presuming that he will be heard.

Well, he won't be heard. Not today. Bravery takes his place at the table. He quietly settles himself down and makes himself at home. I can't hear self-doubt any more. He's burnt himself out. And I'm glad about that, because me and bravery? We've got work to do.

I am going to tell my story.

I am going to write it in a book …

*Three years later …*

**Diary entry, January 2018**
It's Friday evening and I'm lying stretched out on my living room floor with newspapers and magazines scattered all around me. I have a small and sadly ever-decreasing pile of Quality Street chocolates to my right, which is offset by a miniature pot of untouched M&S super green salad to my left. The disparity seems both crude and predictable, but I'm okay with that.

My life hasn't been normal for approximately one week now. I've already come to terms with the challenges of being a reluctant extrovert and my initial apprehension at facing this inevitability courtesy of sharing my story in the pages of a book. But the shocking thing is the degree to which I am successfully pulling it off. Nobody is more surprised than I am. 'You sounded so relaxed during the Marathon Talk interview, Rach.' 'Great job!' 'This interview is brilliant, Rachel!' 'Well done!' 'You were fab!' 'Totally nailed it.'

And so it goes on ...

I've heard from old schoolfriends, childminders, long-lost cousins and workmates from two decades ago. I've been spoken to by the one mum in the school playground I hoped *wouldn't* acknowledge my existence, and quizzed about my PR schedule in a Halifax nail bar, where an old lady sat listening in bemused silence, picking up on the words 'mental health' only to interject with, 'Some bloke threw himself off the motorway bridge last week, didn't he? Poor soul.' Silence ensued.

But on a manageable scale, and in a very – *very* – small way, my story is impacting on people. I know it. I can feel it. As those people who have (and many more who haven't) known me read my words on the page and hear my voice, I get the distinct feeling that I'm not alone – and I can't tell you the joy that brings me. To know that all the years of sadness, madness and quiet, invisible lostness didn't count for nothing; that my efforts to pull myself back from the brink of despair and discover that my story *matters* – hear that again: TO KNOW THAT IT MATTERS – means everything to me.

This is when I begin to realise ...

I was *never* alone.

**Three years later ...**

**June 2021**
It's a strange feeling – like a deep sense of knowing that something isn't quite right. Perhaps in reality it's been building for a long time, but I get a sense that something is about to break. The pains in my legs have been getting worse and growing more and more intense – I've recently described them to various medical professionals as 'shooting pains' or like a constant, uncomfortable fizzing sensation firing up and down the backs of my legs. Not to mention the fact that I feel cold all the time. I hadn't really thought about any of that ... until now.

I've been put in contact with a highly regarded sports coach who immediately advises me to have some blood tests. 'Really?' I ask him, as though it's the most preposterous idea in the world, but I guess he's right – we do need to take a look at what's happening *underneath the bonnet* (I do love a body/car-maintenance analogy).

I immediately make arrangements for some private blood tests, but this has already set my mind spinning on an endless loop of 'what-ifs'. What if something *is* wrong with me? What if they find that something isn't working as it should? I've never fully contemplated that there might be an underlying issue here – which sounds ridiculous, I know. What's worse is that my mind has now exploded with a series of runaway 'worst case scenario' outcomes and I can only see the most unhelpful, unlikely eventualities.

Nothing happens quickly enough. These things take time. Firstly, I have to wait a few days for the DIY blood-testing kit to arrive through the post, and then I must make my own arrangements to visit a friend who is medically qualified and can take the blood samples for me. I have no idea how crazy this runaway trail will become, or where it will lead me.

In the meantime, my diary is crammed full of Zoom calls with runners who want to share their stories with me. I can't help but wonder why this is happening now. It must be for a reason. Every time I speak to one of these people and hear about their experiences it leaves me with a sense of running's incredible power to help people overcome pretty much anything that life could throw at a person. All while my own body feels to be falling apart.

With the prospect of uncertainty looming over my own health, I find myself being captivated by Carly's story and how she survived two breast cancer diagnoses. I am utterly absorbed in my discussion with James as I learn about his mental health struggles throughout his treatment for testicular cancer and the years beyond, when omnipresent fear of the unthinkable replaced what were once happy, cancer-free thoughts.

In recent years I have heard from people who have read about my experiences and feel they have been helped in some way by my sharing them in the pages of a book. But this is like complete role reversal. I am now the one being supported. I am the one benefiting from sitting with my headphones on and listening to these people – fabulous, brave, extraordinary and yet entirely *ordinary* people who have found a way to overcome adversity and to not only survive, but do far more than that. These are people who have chosen to live fiercely and to be fully alive. They are no longer content with the alternative.

Meeting these people and hearing their stories is inspiring and life-affirming, and it gives me every reason to believe that whatever is happening to me 'underneath the bonnet', it will be possible for me to not only survive it (remember we are in 'worst case scenario' catastrophising mental health free-falling territory here) but to *thrive*. That is easy to write but not so easy to do in practice, as I will soon discover. Theory is always a sod in that sense. I don't know how or why, but I get a definite sense that these incredible people are helping me in some way. I am gaining strength by hearing their stories.

\*\*\*

It's fair to say that everything has changed. My running has changed and the reason *why* I run has changed.

Initially, I ran because I wanted to get away from a version of myself that I hated. I wanted to run away from the excessive weight and the self-loathing; to escape the name-calling and the shitty relationships.

Many years later, I ran to regain my identity and perhaps even to create a new one on the other side of motherhood. I've banged on about that journey in another book, but the reason I ran was to prove to myself and my daughter that motherhood wouldn't eat me up and spit me out. I ran to show myself that I could be physically and mentally strong – perhaps even stronger – on the other side.

And then for a long while I ran to feed my incessant running ego. I raced most weekends and achieved some pretty fast times* (*subjectivity caveats apply). No matter how much anxiety I felt about my running, no matter how utterly consumed I was with fear over the outcome, I would push on and on, demanding more and more of my body.

That didn't end well.

At the beginning of the Covid pandemic, running became a sanctuary for me. It became a way for me and my daughter, Tilly, to connect, and it became an escape from the shock of our normal lives dissolving right in front of our eyes.

At the same time, the races stopped. There wasn't the same opportunity for me to constantly feed my running ego. It made me reconnect with running and realise that I don't need the outcomes or the PBs to validate me. I began to realise that the day-to-day joy I feel from running far surpasses those brief glimpses of personal glory.

And although I'm not saying there isn't a place for goal-setting and dream-chasing, I realised that for me to have an ongoing, lasting relationship with running, I can only do that without the fear. I am so done with waking up in a cold sweat in the middle of the night before a Parkrun, completely terrified about how many seconds off my PB I might be in the morning. I am done with the unhealthy connection I used to make between my race performance on any given day and my self-worth. I decided that my relationship with running will be based on joy. None of my running achievements will ever be taken away from me, but along with those there are many horrible memories of fear, dread and crippling anxiety which I can honestly live without.

I made a deal with myself: if I can't enjoy my running journey and take pleasure in the process, then I shouldn't be on the journey at all.

And then came my recent health issues, which included low iron levels and a herniated disc in my lumbar spine.

Having lived with all the different running versions of myself, I am inspired more than ever by the stories of everyday runners just like me. I want to try and understand what it is about running that works for us. How does it make the challenges of life seem ever so slightly more surmountable? What do we have in common and how are the threads of our running stories familiar, even when our life experiences might be so very different? Why is running such a sanctuary for us? How does running help us in big and little ways?

It is an understatement to say that running has changed me, but that is only half the story. The person who emerged on the other side of running wasn't the finished product. Even after the heartbreak of losing running in 2017, as hard as I tried, nothing else felt the same. Nothing filled the gap that running had left. In coming to understand and see running in a completely new light, in the dawning of the *real* reason why I run and the daily joy it brings me, it has enabled me to let go of a version of myself that almost caused me to lose running entirely, and my mental wellbeing in the process.

This is a collection of running stories that inspire me. These people are not celebrities or elite athletes, but real people who are living ordinary lives. Like me, they go about their daily business and have collectively experienced every imaginable obstacle in life which might ordinarily throw a person into a downward spiral. Thankfully, that hasn't happened. Instead, each one of these incredible individuals has found solace in running, as I have learnt to do. In appreciating the real power of running to help us manage everything from day-to-day mental health struggles to all-consuming grief, this is my way of saying thank you to those people who continue to remind me of all that I have learnt along the way.

# CHARLOTTE

The email arrives in my inbox in January 2018. It's one of many hundreds I will receive over the coming weeks and months. I'm new to this. My first book, *Running for My Life*, was only published a handful of days ago, and already it's opened the floodgates that will ultimately lead me here: to the place where sharing *my* story becomes about other people sharing theirs. I will learn that I'm not alone, and that running goes hand-in-hand with incredible stories around mental health challenges, survival and recovery. I will hear from people who have suffered mental breakdowns, bereavements, life-threatening illnesses and, devastatingly, even the loss of a child. I will receive letters from those who find running a way of managing the voice of their 'Bastard Chimp' which threatens to rob them of their daily joy. Parents will connect with me – those who find running helps them to process the endless pressures and anxieties that come hand-in-hand with parenthood and the feelings of complete overwhelm at being responsible for another little life. I will hear from people who are on Prozac and other mental health medication, and some who are recovering from eating disorders such as anorexia and bulimia.

Every one of us has a unique story to tell, but we all have one thing in common: running has helped us in some way. Whatever the circumstance, however our personal demons have manifested, however the dice have rolled and on whatever side they have landed, putting on a pair of running shoes has healed us all. It is the one thing that binds us – holding us together like spider silk: virtually invisible, but stronger than steel.

But I'm unprepared. I am completely unprepared for this.

*Dear Rachel,*

*My name is Charlotte, and I'm twenty-five years old. I live with my parents and I'm suffering with depression. For as long as I can remember, I have battled daily with anxiety, feelings of always failing at life and believing that I'm nothing but a disappointment to myself and those around me.*

*Six years ago, I ran a 5k Race for Life in memory of my nan, and two years ago I completed the British Heart Foundation's May marathon – I completed the marathon equivalent number of miles in a month.*

*Since then, my mental health has gone downhill. I have gained two stone; I am badly depressed; I struggle with everyday life and have suicidal thoughts. I've been trying to find a way to fight it for the sake of my family, and then I stumbled across your book. I cried at the end when you completed your marathon journey. I can relate to you and your story so much with my daily struggles, as I too suffer with that bad voice in my head – the one you refer to as your 'Bastard Chimp'.*

*Yesterday morning I had a meltdown, crying hysterically whilst feeling like I was in physical pain, and I can't go on. My parents are struggling to cope with me, and they don't know what to do to help. They begged me to find an internal fight. And then yesterday, as I came close to finishing reading your story, I took a step forward.*

*While I was slumped on the sofa feeling sorry for myself, I took a leap of faith, and I entered the ballot for the Great North Run. I must be mad! If I'm successful in getting a place I don't know how I will do it, but I wanted to let you know anyway.*

*Thank you for helping me to take a small step forward, even if it is just entering the ballot. I feel like that is a start and, as you know, it's a long road ahead. I know it is going to be incredibly hard and it terrifies me, but thanks to reading your story I have taken my first step in fighting these demons I face every single day.*

*Tomorrow I plan to blow the cobwebs off my running shoes and go out – even if it's just for a walk, it's a start.*

*You have inspired me, and I just wanted to take the time to thank you! Thank you, Rachel. I too will now begin to run for my life.*
*Charlotte*

I am stunned. I have no words. I don't know how to handle this emotional outpouring sent to me by a stranger who is currently in the grip of their own mental health demons – a person who has read about my journey, discovering that running helped me to find a way out.

I don't know why she has reached out to me in this way. What was it about my story that made her want to open up to me about hers? I am here, at the other end of an invisible rope which binds us. Both of us know about mental health suffering. Both of us know how it feels to believe yourself to be entirely unfit for purpose. *'You can't do it.'* … *'Look at you!'* … *'You're just a sad, pathetic mess.'* I've heard those words so many times before, just as Charlotte hears them now. They once taunted me – just like they are taunting her. Maybe that's it. Perhaps that's why she has reached out to me.

The email occupies my mind like a whiteboard that won't wipe clean. I can't get the words out of my head, or the fact that this person – this complete stranger – has connected with me in this unfathomable way.

*Dear Charlotte,*

*I have so much to say to you as I sit here cross-legged on my living room floor having just crawled in through the front door after putting myself on the start line of a race for the umpteenth time since that initial marathon journey you have just been reading about.*

*I'm the usual cocktail of post-race emotions. I'm tired yet full of energy, but more than anything else I feel proud. I am proud of facing up to those horrible, toxic thoughts that tell me I shouldn't even bother turning up to a race in the first place because I have no right to be there. Once again, I've won.*

*And then I read your email …*

*Perhaps it is you seeing the tiniest chink of light in a very dark place, discovering that you have a new friend in the world – one whom you have never even met. It is you reaching out and holding somebody's hand in the loneliest moments and them telling you that you are – and you can be – stronger than you ever imagined possible. It is every single reason why I wrote my book, and although I'm afraid I don't have any miracle cures for you, it was always my hope that somebody just like you would pick up my book, read my story and know that recovery from that dark place is possible.*

*Please know that running ISN'T and MUSTN'T be seen as a 'quick fix' for all mental health demons. In the very early, darkest days of my own struggles, I needed professional help. As you probably know, I was prescribed anti-depressant medication, and I fully believe that was absolutely vital in keeping me from being swept off a cliff of hopelessness and despair. I would urge you to go and seek similar help, and to do it now. You don't have to struggle alone, and you don't need to isolate yourself from the world. It's a different place now to when I was at my lowest ebb. Please tell me you will do that. Make an appointment to see your GP and discuss with them your thoughts and feelings – even if it sounds muddled, confused and you don't know where to begin. Just start somewhere …*

*Secondly, I applaud you for taking those other incremental steps towards a brighter, happier place. You have already felt the positive effects of completing the Race for Life, and you can do that again. In entering the ballot for the Great North Run, you have chosen what I realise must seem like an enormously scary and intimidating goal, but it IS possible. You CAN get yourself to the start line, and you CAN run/jog/walk/crawl over the finish line, too …*

I go and make myself a cup of tea – I need to take a breather. I'm a complete newbie to the whole 'publishing your life story in a book' party, and I have no idea how to respond. Something about Charlotte's story affects me so deeply, I can almost feel her straining for help, trying desperately to reach out her fingertips as though she is caught in the turbulence of the worst mental health maelstrom, and she is using every ounce of strength to grab hold of a life raft which is almost within grasp. It makes me wonder – is that what I am? A life raft? But surely that can't be right. I've only written a story about my own experiences. I'm not a counsellor or a therapist, or somebody who has any professional knowledge of helping a person like Charlotte – someone who is experiencing serious mental health illness.

I struggle to switch my mind off. What do I do with this now?

> *... What's more, Charlotte, I will run the Great North Run with you. Although there are no guarantees for either of us, it is my hope that we can run/jog/walk – or crawl – across the finish line of the Great North Run 2018 together.*
>
> *You have just made a new long-distance friend, and I will support you on your journey.*
>
> *So, thank you for getting in touch with me and for being brave.*
>
> *I look forward to hearing your progress and please know that I am championing you daily from my Yorkshire home. Take the steps I mentioned above – please see your GP and keep reaching out for the help and the support that you need, just like you have done by contacting me.*
>
> *All being well, I will see you in Newcastle on 9 September.*
> *With my very best wishes,*
> *Rachel Ann Cullen*

Of course, in hindsight, my email response to Charlotte is completely inappropriate. I am unable to stop myself from taking on the emotional burden and responsibility of another person's pain and absorbing it as though it were my own. I can't comprehend the fact that I am not – nor should I expect myself to be – the answer to Charlotte's troubles. I can't accept that the burden of her recovery doesn't lie with me. She is not in my hands simply by virtue of her reading my story. Her mental wellbeing is not mine to manage or to resolve.

Nonetheless, I have offered to run the 2018 Great North Run with Charlotte and I have applied for a place in the public ballot. *This is complete madness!* I press send on my email response, but inside I know that I cannot simply offer myself up as a hand-holding race partner for each broken person who reaches out to share their story with me.

My gut feeling is correct. Before long, I find myself embroiled in Charlotte's increasing emotional turbulence. A few days after our initial email exchange, I receive this.

*Hi Rachel,*

*I'm sorry to tell you that I'm really struggling. Everyone keeps saying that I need to start running if I have any hope of completing the Great North Run, and already it's putting a lot of pressure on me. I think my best friend understands. She said, 'Who said you have to run it all, anyway?' and I guess she's right.*

*Today I snapped again at my partner over his lack of help around the house. Little things like that affect me a lot and I have slapped him in the past with outbursts of rage. I didn't hit him today, but I exploded with anger, screaming and crying. He told me that he was going to move out, but I pleaded with him not to leave me. He said that he was not leaving me – just simply moving out for a little while. I don't think he knows how to cope with my emotional outbursts any more.*

*This weekend I have fallen off the wagon and I've just eaten my feelings. And I haven't mentioned this previously, but I have recently been thinking about having a baby, although I know that now is not exactly the right time. I think I'm just at that age where my hormones are through the roof. I'm sorry to burden you with this stuff.*
*Charlotte*

Suddenly it dawns on me. Emotionally, I am increasingly feeling like a leaky bucket. This is all too much. Talk of domestic abuse, self-harm, thoughts of having a baby while in the middle of a mental health crisis … and as much as I am willing myself to be there for this person, I am capsizing. There simply isn't enough room in my head for me to manage my own mental health needs and those of every single person who might want to share their burdens with me.

I wonder: what on earth have I done? Is this what sharing my story means? Am I simply an emotional sponge put out on public display to absorb other people's pain?

I become increasingly concerned for Charlotte's welfare. I begin to wonder if she has harmed herself in some way, or whether the people she has surrounding her are aware of the depths of her pain. I know enough to be worried, but I am simply too far away to be able to help. Charlotte drifts into my thoughts when there is a lull at work and in the quiet moments before sleep arrives.

I don't hear from her again.

The reason for my sharing this story is because at one time – and for a very long time – I honestly didn't think that my story mattered. The Bastard Chimp would rear his ugly head at frequent intervals and remind me, 'So fucking what, Rachel? Who cares?' The email from Charlotte was perhaps the first time I was forced to consider the prospect that my story *did* matter; my story *does* matter. Not because there is anything extraordinary about my experiences or achievements. There are no Olympic gold medals, FKTs or Guinness World Records to speak of. I am by no means the fastest female to run any specified distance, although I have had my fair share of personal 'wow!' moments courtesy of my own running accomplishments. But the realisation that my story *mattered* to another human being was huge.

And from that place, it began to dawn on me that perhaps there are many of us who don't believe our stories to be worth sharing. We get up every morning and go about our business; we put on our trainers, and we run. We turn up at races filled with anxiety and pose for exhilarated, salt-crusted selfies at the end, imagining that none of it matters – that it's unimportant. We see social media posts of ultra-athletes hop-skipping for hundreds of sleep-deprived miles across mountainous terrain; we see those who are not content with running one marathon, so they choose to tackle some incomprehensible number back-to-back. We are faced with the prospect that they are made of sterner stuff than we are – that they are superhuman in some way. And it's funny, because as incredible as some of those individuals and their feats are, they are not the ones which impact on me the most.

The truth is, our stories *do* matter. Everyday stories of overcoming adversity, battling fear and the taunts of the Bastard Chimp who would have us believe that running isn't for us. The stories of bravery which are born in taking those very first tentative steps out of the front door. For me, bravery doesn't need to involve taking on outlandish feats or incomprehensible goals. And it's not to say that progression isn't something to aim for or be proud of – I more than anyone know how incredible that feels – but running is about so much more than that.

The spider silk of running binds us because we understand that running helps us. It enables us to silence the chimp and write another story for ourselves – one where things become *possible*. This is what I want to explore. It is why I want to share your stories – because we are all, in a sense, running for our lives.

I think it's also important to stress that all the stories told within this book are deeply personal accounts. Each of the individuals who have chosen to be open and talk to me about their experiences hasn't done so to represent an entire group of people, or to be a voice for one particular struggle. I say this because I know from personal experience how choosing to be brave and talk about your struggles opens you up to judgement and criticism, and I want to be clear from the outset that these people are *not* spokespersons. Like me, they don't claim to represent everyone who might have travelled along the same or even a similar route to them; they have simply chosen to share their own experiences. Nowadays, social media can be a cruel place and, sadly, there are always people who are ready to jump on to others and be outraged for one reason or another. My hope is that you, the reader, don't interpret things in this way. One individual's experience of living with cancer, body dysmorphia, grief, baby loss, an eating disorder or any other life struggle is just that. It is *one person's experience*. It is nothing more and should not be interpreted as such.

And so, I consider that all these people are incredibly brave to put themselves forward and to open themselves up in this way. It is certainly not an easy thing to do. There will always be somebody who is quick to judge and slow to comprehend the strength and dignity it takes to be honest and vulnerable about an aspect of your life. In my mind we should be sensitive about another person's struggle and their story, because nobody should be made to feel ashamed of what they have lived through.

# I RUN THIS BODY!

I feel like a rabbit caught in a trap. It's 1998 and I'm on a treadmill at the university gym campus and, as usual, I feel compelled to run but at the same time I am desperate to escape from here. As much as the metronomic sound of my feet striking the running belt is rhythmical and strangely soothing for my head, the image of my chest bouncing lopsidedly in the full-length mirror ahead of me is crippling. And it isn't just the image that taunts me, but the physical reminder I feel with every single wretched step.

I am nineteen years old; I am suffering with disordered eating and compulsive exercising, and I am now in the firm grip of body dysmorphia, resulting from the fact that after some recent weight loss (largely due to running very moderate distances on a regular basis) it has become very apparent that I have asymmetrical breasts.

One of the worst ways in which this affects my daily life is the impact on my mental health and my physical freedom to run. I say that not because there is any reason why I *can't* run as effectively or efficiently with one breast two cup-sizes bigger than the other, but psychologically I am filled with terror about other people's judgements of my flawed, unfit-for-purpose teenage body while the running movement exaggerates the discrepancy.

I fantasise about being able to wear a normal bra and a skinny T-shirt without being tormented by the eyes of other girls gawping at my chest, in my mind no doubt asking themselves, 'Is it just the light, or is one of Rachel's tits bigger than the other?'

Any which way I look at it, this is affecting me on such a deep psychological level and in all aspects of my life. My university studies are suffering; I have developed an eating disorder; I am constantly distracted from even the simplest things; and, worst of all, it has distanced me from the girls I live with. I am so ashamed of my physical defect that – whether or not they have worked it out for themselves – I refuse to confide in any of them. I am simply too embarrassed and too filled with hatred of my own body. It has let me down once again with wonky, saggy tits that wouldn't look out of place on an eighty-year-old woman. I am beyond frustrated, a long way past disappointed, but I am absolutely *nowhere near* acceptance.

I am determined to see to it that my physical flaw is rectified. I research the options available to me and decide to have bilateral breast reduction and uplift surgery to sculpt my body into the shape of a 'normal' nineteen-year-old girl.

My decision is final – there is no going back.

Some months later, the surgery is complete. I am strapped up like a mummy underneath my T-shirt. It will take many months – many years, in fact – for my bright red, swollen scars to fade from an angry shade of scarlet and to reduce in size, eventually melting back into my skin. But I figure that is a price I am willing to pay to feel normal while running on a treadmill and wearing a skinny T-shirt.

Over the years, I will think about my choices and consider that this was the right decision for me to make at the time. I will always be thankful for having the option of reconstructive surgery, allowing me to finally be able to run in peace and to wear my summer T-shirts in a beer garden without silently writhing around in my own skin.

However …

Fast-forward twenty-three years. I am now forty-three years old. The mental health journey I have undertaken has been a long and difficult one – especially when running fell apart for me in 2017 and body dysmorphia came back to hit me so hard that I could barely breathe with the ferocity of its gut-wrenching blow.

I have since undertaken some very successful cognitive behavioural therapy to help with the management of the condition. But at times I wonder if my intense hatred of my flawed young body and my desire to remedy it and replace the 'bad' parts of myself through surgery was a precursor for body dysmorphia to set in and take firm hold. I wonder if the fact that I was simply unable to accept myself as I was, and to settle with the fact that I might have to wear modified bras or slightly alter my style of clothing, was indicative of my vulnerability to the condition which went on to ravage me for decades. I will never know …

It is autumn 2020. I am mindlessly scrolling through Instagram when a face pops up on my feed. I don't know the face, but I am completely stunned by her radiance. And although of course the concept of beauty is entirely subjective, I happen to believe that this woman is absolutely *beautiful*, and I cannot explain the joy and the *life* she radiates through the virtual metropolis that is social media. You see, it isn't just a photograph of her face that I am looking at, but of the scars that now lie where her breasts used to be. I see her standing there looking so fucking beautiful and radiant *without any breasts* and with a smile that could end wars. Who is this woman? I need to know more.

It is Breast Cancer Awareness Month and Carly – the beautiful, breastless woman – has posted on social media encouraging other women to be vigilant and look out for any slight changes to their breasts. She is well placed to make this appeal, as she has experienced breast cancer not once but twice, ultimately resulting in a bilateral mastectomy in April 2020 – right at the beginning of a global pandemic.

But this particular post is hidden in amongst hundreds of sweaty (still radiant) running selfies. This woman runs. In fact, her entire family runs. She runs alone; she runs with her husband and with her sons; and she looks … *happy*. She looks so fucking happy I want to bottle it and sell it, thereby ending a global misery pandemic.

What fascinates me about Carly is not only the deep joy and the real beauty she exudes, but the fact that her incredible journey with breast cancer is not the main focus of her social media platform. It takes its place behind the great loves of her life – her family and running. Cancer doesn't run the show in Carly's life; her joy for living does.

And as a person who has been so badly affected by body dysmorphia – a mental health condition which mercifully doesn't have a possible death sentence attached to it yet still manages to gnaw away at a person's daily joy – I find it incredible to see Carly and to know that for her, not only doesn't she particularly *mind* that both her breasts have been removed, but in some ways she celebrates the fact. I want to know how this is possible and what I can learn from Carly following her experiences and her outlook on life. What role has running played in her ability to process the two cancer diagnoses she has lived through? Has it impacted on her decision to reject the option for reconstructive surgery? If so, then how, and why?

In a world where so much value is placed on aesthetics and women are judged – and we judge ourselves – according to a stereotypical kind of perfection, Carly becomes a beacon for an entirely different kind of beauty. And to be clear, I am not comparing the different experiences we have lived or suggesting that a mental health illness is in any way comparable to a cancer diagnosis – that would be ridiculous. Nor am I minimising the impact of a condition such as body dysmorphia. Although rational thought would have me feeling thoroughly ashamed for the futility of my suffering, mental health illness is not concerned with rational thought. It will eat you up regardless.

Just as Carly had her cancerous lumps removed, I took affirmative action to free myself from my toxic thoughts. One is not comparable to another. But sharing stories of our own experiences – as women and as runners – surely helps us to see things from a different perspective …

# CARLY

Her face lights up the screen. The truth is, there is *so much* I want to talk to Carly about, I'm not quite sure where to begin. I guess a good place to start is the thing that binds us: running.

Carly tells me that she began running seventeen years ago. With the incessant demands of young children snapping at her heels, she found herself struggling with motherhood. 'I found it completely exhausting,' she says. 'I didn't feel like I was doing a great job and everyone else around me seemed to be enjoying motherhood far more than I was. It was tough.'

A buzzer goes off in my head, rather like a bingo caller shouting out a number that matches mine. *Me too!* I know that same terrifying sense of overwhelm as a new mum. Perhaps I had a premonition that I might struggle with the mental health implications of all the responsibility and newness and the fact that I might no longer be able to identify myself or my own life in the muddy tangle of motherhood, and so that is why, during the early stages of my pregnancy, I set myself the goal to run the London Marathon in 2010. And just as I was inspired to run that iconic first marathon by watching it on the telly during my sedentary teenage years, I learn that this was also the catalyst for Carly's venture into marathon running. *Bingo again!* Carly tells me that she remembers watching the London Marathon coverage on the BBC with her husband, and when she saw tens of thousands of people of all possible shapes, sizes and ages taking part, she figured, 'Well, if they can do it, then so can I!' The next words she said to her husband were, 'Do you fancy running the London Marathon with me?'

Her lovely husband, Matt, who Carly describes as 'Mr Laidback', replied, 'Yeah, sure!' So the very next day they both went out for a run – or a jog – only to predictably die after a few hundred metres, as she recalls. But as hard as that very first outing was, something made them both go out again the next day, and then the next. 'We built up to running a few miles without stopping and kept going from there,' she says. When Carly was able to run for four miles continuously, she recalls a sense of true joy at the realisation that something seismic had happened to her. Something had changed in her psychology, and she realised that running made her feel not just good, but amazing! It was – in her words – transformational.

From there, running became a part of Carly's daily life. Matt would come home from work and walk into a house filled with the sound of boisterous toddlers, and Carly would take herself straight out for a run. She tells me that she felt like a changed person when she came back in through the front door. 'I felt calm and happy after a run, whereas before I discovered running, I used to cry and feel exhausted, sobbing "I can't do this!" to Matt.'

Unlike me, Carly doesn't consider that she was suffering from a mental health illness at the time, but believes that she needed something to give her a brief escape from the incessant demands of motherhood and to feel good about herself again. She says that running allowed her to believe that she was 'good enough': a good enough person, and a good enough mum. In short, it gave her self-belief. Carly secured a place in the London Marathon that year, and it changed the course of her life.

Carly and I are the same age. Our life experiences may be very different, but our stories already have one major commonality: the feeling of complete overwhelm as a new mum. I have one daughter, whereas Carly has four children – but running has helped us both to mentally process the daily challenges of parenthood. On that, we unite. Carly says that she wishes she had started running earlier in her life, and she now credits running with her ability to know with deep conviction that she isn't just a good mum but a great one. She doesn't say that in a bombastic, arrogant manner; just in the context of being a strong and confident mother who is giving her children some of the most valuable tools with which they can navigate their own way through the many challenges of life. Running is undoubtedly one of the most effective weapons that Carly has discovered, and she is now passing it on to her children. She is teaching them how to build a solid base of physical fitness, mental wellbeing and self-esteem. 'I've had some really special runs when both my boys and their friends have run with me,' she says. 'It's so important to me that my boys run, as I know how much it will help with their mental health in the future.'

We've been talking for well over half an hour before we even mention the 'C' word: cancer. Or, more specifically, breast cancer.

Let's break this down into its two component parts. Firstly, breasts. I talk to Carly about my experience as a young woman with raging body dysmorphia and the breast reduction surgery I had, aged nineteen. I say that her story resonates so strongly with me from the perspective of body image and mental health, and I'm fascinated to know if and how running has played a part in her decision not to have her breasts reconstructed following a bilateral mastectomy resulting from two cancer diagnoses. There is no purpose in even attempting to align a mental health illness such as body dysmorphia with the impact of cancer, but there is something about the effect on us both as women in dealing with and managing conditions which have directly impacted on our bodies – and our mental health – in such a fundamental and profound way.

On to the second component part: cancer. Aged thirty-one, Carly discovered a small lump beside her right breast somewhere close to her armpit, courtesy of her young daughter's tiny hand as it explored her mother's body while crawling over her in bed one morning. Although it was only a pea-sized lump, immediately and instinctively Carly knew what it was. She took the necessary steps and discovered that the cancer was only small – six millimetres in size – and, mercifully, in the very early stages. She tells me that she never had a 'why me?' kind of feeling following the diagnosis. Sounding very matter of fact, Carly talks me through the subsequent cancer treatment. She underwent a lumpectomy and a course of radiotherapy. It didn't seem like such a big deal to her at the time. This was just a thing that happened to her which needed dealing with swiftly so that she could get on with her life. In Carly's mind, she was one of the lucky ones.

Carly talks about the aftermath of the first cancer diagnosis: the lumpectomy and the fact that she wasn't particularly fearful of the cancer returning, although she accepted that it probably would. Most recurrent cancers appear within the first two or three years after treatment, but in some cases the cancer can recur many years later. According to the Susan G. Komen organisation, 'women with early breast cancer most often develop local recurrence within the first five years after treatment. On average, seven to eleven per cent of women with early breast cancer experience a local recurrence during this time.'[1] And so, Carly set about coming to terms with that possibility in her own mind. At that time, she also began to prepare herself for the prospect of a double mastectomy at some point in her future life. She did her homework. She researched every aspect of her potential reality, familiarising herself with the appearance of scars replacing breasts and informing herself of the statistical likelihood of her facing that very same outcome. Like marathon running, preparation is key, and Carly did the groundwork.

Carly tells me that she wasn't freaked out or devastated by the sight of a female chest without any breasts. Instead, she thought, 'I'll take that for another ten or twenty years of my life.' All the while, she recounted the many things for which she was thankful, and tells me that while she was considering the undeniably real prospect of the cancer returning, her overriding mindset was one of deep gratitude. 'I've lived a fabulous and blessed life, so how could I possibly moan?' Carly's positive outlook and her ability to reframe her situation and focus on all the good in her life is astounding. When it would have been so easy to allow fear and uncertainty to trample all over her headspace, she chose an alternative: gratitude. If I wasn't already, I am now completely in awe.

How did running help Carly during this time? I can't help but imagine that the young mum who was struggling to cope with toddlers – the woman who hadn't discovered that running could help her in so many ways – might have had a very different outlook to a cancer diagnosis from the Carly I am talking with today. Carly is convinced that running has enabled her to remain strong both physically and mentally throughout her experiences, but says that she will never know the full answer to that question. The simple truth is that the young woman who struggled so much with the newness of motherhood wasn't the same person dealing with a cancer diagnosis: a stronger, more resilient, mentally robust Carly was.

In offering a balanced view of her circumstances, Carly tells me of the other aspects of her life that have influenced her ability to deal with adversity. I learn that her dad was an incredibly positive person who taught her to appreciate the little things in life and to feel grateful for what she had, rather than dwelling on the things she didn't. Carly is also quick to mention her lovely husband, Matt, and to credit him and their rock-solid twenty-year relationship with giving her some of that self-belief and acceptance. 'I didn't do this alone,' she says. 'Matt has been there throughout all of it, and he's made me feel beautiful regardless. He's never tried to change me.' Her eyes light up on mentioning his name. 'Matt and the running together helped me to build up my self-confidence.'

I've heard so many stories of unhealthy partnerships and of deep-rooted insecurities causing damage within a relationship, but this is the antidote to all that. Carly's children have seen first-hand how a truly supportive relationship together with a firm base of self-esteem has empowered their mum and has subsequently helped all of them to live with joy and gratitude every single day.

It is March 2020, eleven years after Carly's diagnosis. Covid-19 is just beginning to sink its dirty claws into the entire globe. In the space of one week, Carly will experience a swing of emotions huge enough to cause even the strongest foundation to be shaken to its core. At the start of the week, she runs her own virtual marathon from home, as the one she has been training for has been cancelled. Guess what? She doesn't waste any time ruminating about what might have been. 'It was such a truly fantastic day,' she joyfully recalls, with tales of her husband and children running with her for certain parts of the route, and – as usual – a beaming smile spreads across her face. Listening to her, I can't help but wish I'd been there.

Less than twenty-four hours later, a national lockdown came into force and Carly's annual mammogram was scheduled for the very next day. All of a sudden, the endorphin-filled virtual marathon seemed light years away.

She half expected her routine appointment to be cancelled due to the pandemic, and she tells me that she even considered cancelling it herself, not wanting to 'waste' vital NHS resources at such a challenging time. Only at the very last minute did she decide to stick to her scheduled review. Carly describes the incredible and monumental efforts of the NHS staff to enable that routine mammogram to go ahead. And it's a bloody good job it did.

This time, there was no lump, no forewarning. Just the statistical likelihood of the cancer returning, which Carly had been contemplating for the previous eleven years. Something concerning came up on the scan, and the consultant wanted to perform an emergency biopsy right there and then. There was no time to waste. Carly had planned on running home from the hospital appointment on that day, but instead, she had to phone Matt and ask him for a lift following the sudden turn of events. Once again, she knew instinctively what the outcome would be.

Two weeks went by, and the consultant telephoned Carly, informing her that they had indeed found another low-grade cancer in her breast. This time, the lump measured five millimetres in size – slightly smaller than the first one. Carly was fast-tracked for a series of full-body scans to establish if the cancer had spread elsewhere. Mercifully, those tests came back clear. With confirmation that her life wasn't in imminent danger, she set about the prospect of having a second cancerous lump removed from her breast.

Following two experiences of cancer in the same breast, Carly told the NHS consultant that she wanted to have both breasts removed. However, the response she received took her back a little. The consultant informed Carly that they couldn't remove both breasts: they were only able to operate on the breast which had been affected by the cancer. 'That was the only time I felt like a cancer patient,' Carly tells me, and for the first time, I see her smile completely disappear. It wasn't just about the *look* of her breasts, but it was more about the *feel* of her body. And, more importantly, how it felt to run. Carly says this was a huge part of her decision-making at this critical moment in her life. She wanted to feel at peace with her body. She wanted to be able to continue to do the thing she loves the most. She wanted to run.

'I know that many women might find that strange,' she says. 'Boobs are a fundamental part of what makes you a woman, but they honestly don't matter to me.' As she is talking, I notice that the smile is creeping back on to her face. She acknowledges the impact on her husband, saying that at times she feels for Matt, who she presumes is missing out a little. But I look at that smile and wonder if the thought has ever crossed his mind. My guess is that it hasn't.

Carly told the NHS consultant that she simply couldn't face having just one breast removed. She insisted that she wanted a double mastectomy and pleaded with them to allow her to make this decision about her own body. Due to the unfortunate timing – being right at the start of a global pandemic – and because of the many hoops she would be required to jump through to evidence the sanity of her decision, she was advised that it could take anything up to a year for that to happen, if it happened at all. Carly describes this moment as being her 'mini breakdown'. Mentally, she had felt strong throughout both cancer diagnoses. Resolute. Never wavering. Simply taking the next logical steps forward while trying to process her own reality. But when faced with the prospect of her wish for a bilateral mastectomy being delayed or even refused completely, Carly sank into a place of despair for the first time. She wanted to be able to live the rest of her days without mental anguish and a permanent reminder of her cancer. To remove one breast would leave her feeling like – in her words – a 'cancer victim'. To remove both would leave her feeling like a woman who had made her own choices. The difference is stark.

Carly is quick to emphasise that everybody's story is different, and she would hate to offend anyone who has made or would make a different decision in the same circumstances, but this is about her body – and ultimately her life. Carly instinctively knew what she needed to do. 'How am I going to run?' she cried despairingly to Matt. 'How am I going to run like that?' She just wanted both her breasts removing. It really was that simple.

With the NHS no longer a viable option, Carly sought out the double mastectomy surgery she so desperately wanted privately. I ask her about the possibility of breast reconstructive surgery. What options was she given? I want to fully understand her reason for declining this as a possibility. First off, Carly points out that her surgeon was 'absolutely amazing'. She credits her with being a significant part of Carly's speedy recovery. There were multiple Zoom consultations beforehand, and although Carly's surgeon was happy to provide her with the bilateral mastectomy she so desperately wanted, she insisted on exploring all the options – including reconstructive surgery – with her in advance. Carly was also required to have several in-depth consultations with a psychiatrist to evidence that she had researched all available possibilities and had fully considered her position. Remaining resolute, Carly eventually jumped through all the requisite hoops and the date for her surgery was set.

Carly explains that it was her surgeon's fear that with both breasts removed, she might no longer 'feel like a woman'. Being just forty-three years old – still relatively young – Carly was advised to consider the long-term impact of her decision. Would she regret her choice further down the line? Carly fully understood that this was necessary as part of the pre-surgery due diligence, and she was happy to go along with whatever assessments were required in order to establish that her decision was unwavering, fully considered and in her best interests.

I ask Carly if it would be possible for her to go back at a later date and have reconstructive surgery, should she change her mind. She explains that the passage of time makes this prospect more difficult. Skin heals and becomes tighter, making it more challenging to reshape the hollowed-out breast area. Carly immediately rejected the option of breast implants, not wishing to have anything put into her body – it was enough to have parts of it removed. She was given the option of having flesh taken from her stomach area and reconstructed into breasts, but she explains that this would have been a very complex operation with huge implications, not to mention increased risks of infection and a vastly prolonged recovery period. 'At the end of the day, I just wanted to get on with my life and get back running!' she tells me. Carly stuck to her guns, even though she wondered if she would ultimately be coerced into making a different decision – perhaps one that was more easily understood.

Just five weeks after her routine check-up, having finally convinced both her surgeon and the psychiatrist, Carly had the double mastectomy operation one Friday teatime. Unbelievably, she was back home again by Saturday lunchtime. She discovered that she could move her arms more freely than expected as she hadn't needed a drain to be fitted (as is common practice for this type of operation). I ask her how she felt afterwards. Her answer? 'I felt absolutely brilliant! When I woke up and saw that my chest was completely flat, it was the best feeling.'

We discuss the fact that running builds self-belief. Those we love can cheer us on and holler screams of support while handing out orange wedges and energy gels, but there is a sense of self-empowerment gleaned from the indisputable fact that running a marathon is about individual grit, inner strength and absolute doggedness. And although a person can be supported within a relationship or an encouraging training environment, it doesn't alter the fact that your own two feet will ultimately get you across the finish line. Carly believes that this is a great lesson in life.

I have reflected on my discussion with Carly many times and it has made me think about what really matters. Although we have lived through very different experiences, this chat with Carly feels like an echo chamber. Everything she says, I find myself thinking, 'yes … yes … YES!' We have both found the thing we love to do that brings us calm amidst chaos and strength when we are at our most vulnerable. Running might not be the answer for everyone, but in discovering the thing that makes us feel happy and most alive, it has given both me and Carly a sense of freedom and focus in our lives.

Since sharing her story with me, Carly went on to complete a thirty-one-mile ultramarathon in June 2021 – something she describes as being her proudest running achievement. 'I ran the ultramarathon one year after my double mastectomy,' she says. 'I thought my fitness would take a lot longer to come back, but it turns out I was the fittest I've ever been!'

Carly tells me that her future running goals are 'to carry on loving the feeling that running gives me, whether that's the peace of running alone or the connection when I run with my family'. She is already planning to run a longer ultramarathon next year.

# MARTIN

It's 2019 and I am alone at Christmastime. I didn't plan to be, but then sometimes things just happen, don't they? I have some close friends who are checking in on me remotely from their festive family sofas, but I find myself sinking into bouts of sadness that I just can't shift.

The spider silk I have spun over the last ten years begins to work its magic. I receive a text message from a virtual running friend who wants to meet up with me for a run. It reads:

*Hey Rach. Have you checked your diary yet?*

We bonded over our running stories a while back. Arguably, that has been easier for me than most, courtesy of me sharing mine in the pages of a book. But by doing so, it has opened up a whole new world of friendship and support that I'd never imagined. I smile and momentarily forget that I am stuck here, in a hotel room by myself on Christmas Eve.

In amongst the many types of questionable communication I have received over the past four years, I have developed some genuine friendships with people who get me. They understand what running does to help me at times of personal crisis and uncertainty. This is the thread that binds us – however many miles apart – from a hotel room in the Yorkshire Peaks to a living room somewhere on the east coast of England.

A whole year has passed since that woeful solitary Christmas. Our conversation begins effortlessly – like a pair of old friends catching up after lost time. We laugh at the fact that this is the first time we have actually spoken to each other. 'Can you believe it?' we sing in unison. Neither of us can, and yet the only contact we've had is via social media and the occasional supportive text message. 'Some of my best friends I've never even met!' Martin laughs … and he's right. His familiar East Yorkshire accent immediately flings me back a couple of decades to when I was a law student at the University of Hull. 'Five', I soon realised, was pronounced 'farve', and 'nine' became 'narn'. It makes me smile.

I thought I was a relative latecomer to the running party, only discovering the real joy in running aged thirty-three when my first marathon journey began. But Martin was an even later arrival – his running journey beginning somewhat reluctantly in February 2017, aged forty-nine, when a particularly resourceful ex-girlfriend helpfully suggested that he should save on the cost of an expensive gym membership and go out for a run instead. 'I don't even like running,' he replied. Her response? 'How the hell do you know? You haven't even tried!' Martin eventually conceded that she had a valid point.

Like me, when Martin was younger, he hated running – or at least he *thought* he did. 'I used to say to people that I can't see the point of running for running's sake,' he tells me, laughing at his own recollection of the person he used to be.

I wonder which parts of our story are the same. What aspects of our experiences do we share? 'I can't say that I've been through the same as you,' Martin says, 'but I suffered from other mental health issues that I didn't even realise at the time.'

Martin tells me that in the past, he'd always been seen as the 'funny guy' – the life and soul of the party, a good laugh. But all that was just an outer persona. Inside, he was all over the place – a bit like his weight, which yo-yoed dramatically for many years, peaking at just over seventeen stone.

'I was in a turbulent relationship. The only real grounding I had was my work. My family life was volatile and I used alcohol to try and help me level things off. And when my relationship ended, I completely lost myself in booze. I didn't know how much of a mess I was in at the time,' he says. 'You can be in a flux and not realise how bad that place is. I don't think I realised that there was anything wrong with me. I didn't have a clue. Mentally, I was a mess; physically, I was all over the place and I completely lost myself in binge drinking.'

Martin is aware that motherhood was the catalyst for me to set myself a huge running goal for my own physical and mental wellbeing, but what was his turning point? 'My relationship ended, and I was on my own. I felt totally lost at the weekends and I hated being by myself. If no one was going out, then I'd drink by myself at home – but that just felt so ... *sad*. My relationships weren't working out. I bounced from one bad one to another. I finally made a decision that I wouldn't get into another relationship until I could be happy on my own and at peace with myself. One of my friends suggested that I join the local running club. I think lots of people are a bit scared of joining a club, as I was, because they imagine that everyone is Paula Radcliffe and Mo Farah or something. But I went down and discovered it wasn't like that at all.'

Martin had struggled for years in his relationships. He asked himself a question: 'Would *I* be happy going out with me?' It's a fair point! Although grateful for the good friends he'd known over the years, he identified that this was mainly based on socialising down the pub, and he wanted to get away from that being his only source of friendship and emotional support. I remember feeling exactly the same way and choosing to ditch the wine bars and corporate party scene which only exacerbated my sadness, causing untold chaos and damaging my health in the process. Like Martin, I knew that if I had any chance of becoming the person I wanted to be, I needed to find a way of becoming resilient if relationships didn't turn out as I hoped. And so, we both decided to rebuild our lives on different terms.

In our parallel universes, we both set about creating a physical and mental base which was robust and unwavering. We needed to build a platform of inner resilience which didn't depend on external validation from flawed relationships or going out on a weekend bender. We started running and began to discover inner calm. Martin created a joyful life and a strong foundation of wellbeing, and from there he's now going full circle and paying it forward. 'I've been a member of the running club for three years in February,' he tells me, 'and I was made Chairman two weeks ago. I feel like I'm in a place now where I can pass on some of the help I received to other people. That's not saying I know everything about running, but it's about the support, the help and the motivation. I want to do that because I've gained so much. Every day I celebrate feeling fully alive. It's like being reborn as a completely different person,' he beams. 'The Martin I was four years ago wouldn't believe the person I am now or the life I am living today; and the person I am now can barely even comprehend who I was back then.'

I smile, knowing exactly what he means, because we both know how it feels to exist without any of the joy that running has brought us. We've seen things from the other side. I was thirty-three and Martin was forty-nine when we discovered running, and we've both lived more in the years since than in any of the ones that came before.

'I only wish I'd discovered running sooner!' he says. I can't help but agree.

Since sharing his story with me, Martin has gone on to complete the Hardmoors Saltburn Trail Marathon with his partner, Justine (who he met through their mutual love of running). 'It was never about the time,' he says. 'It was always the experience and – oh, my goodness! – the sights along the Cleveland Way and across the North York Moors were incredible!'

Martin has already ticked off a few of his personal running goals, achieving a sub-ninety-minute half marathon and a sub-twenty-minute 5k, and he is now focusing on helping his running club – the Bridlington Road Runners – to develop and continue inspiring others to run. He would also like to break the forty-minute barrier for a 10k and to run the London Marathon someday.

# RUNNING THROUGH GRIEF

It is February 2021 and we are in the midst of the most brutal, seemingly relentless global pandemic. Here in the UK, we're suffering badly. The numbers are bordering on incomprehensible, with the death tally continuing to numb us, day after day. Someone on social media posted a visual representation of the UK's staggering 100,000-plus death toll. It's a mind-boggling image of the 1985 Live Aid concert in Philadelphia with a crowd of over 90,000 people resembling a supersized ant colony (thanks, Google search, for confirming that these colonies do exist). But at the time of writing, even that is about 17,000 people short. Like so many others, I simply can't get my head around the statistics, or the image of an entire stadium packed with people who have since perished.

One thing to note about this pandemic is the cruel reality that this virus is predisposed to killing the elderly – our parents and grandparents. Statistics show that age is the single most important factor for predicting morbidity. According to the Office for National Statistics, for every 100 people who die from Covid-19, eighty-nine of them are over the age of sixty-five.[2] It is a horrifying truth that none of us can ignore.

I'm one of the lucky ones. I've just been for a socially distanced walk with my fit and healthy seventy-six-year-old mum. It's something that we didn't do nearly enough of when times were good and we went about our daily business never imagining that life would change beyond recognition.

'What have you got in your bags?' I ask my mum just as we're about to leave her apartment. I'm wondering why on earth she would need a bulging, oversized handbag plus an enormous rucksack for coming on a gentle walk with me. She doesn't know that today is my rest day – I'm supposed to be allowing my legs to recover after yesterday's tough fartlek training session. I *was* looking forward to a nice steady walk with my mother, but as I look at her standing there with her sturdy walking boots laced up and a rucksack on her back with both buckles now fastened securely across her chest, I'm not so sure.

'I brought over these new walking poles,' I tell her. I've been meaning to try them out for a while now, having seen many serious hikers and ultra-runners using them to help with stability and movement while traversing tricky, off-road terrain.

'Oh,' she replies with more than a whiff of disdain, 'I won't be needing *those* anytime soon.' I know what she's thinking: they're for old people. It's a category she doesn't particularly associate herself with. I get it, but I simply can't erase the image of the packed Live Aid stadium from my mind.

She still hasn't told me what's in the bag.

We set off walking briskly and soon reach the start of the mile-long strenuous incline. I clunk my poles on the ground ahead of me, tapping my way up the hillside as my mother keeps pace, chatting along effortlessly beside me. I can feel my heart beginning to thump loudly in my chest as the path twists and turns ever upwards, but I can't hear my mum breathing heavily – not at all. I glance across and marvel at her level of fitness, which would surely be the envy of people decades younger.

She stops briefly to admire the semi-fluorescent moss which has completely smothered a drystone wall, and again to take in the beauty of some shiny red berries hanging like jewels from a tree part way along the muddy, off-road path. 'I love to imagine the horses coming up here and stopping for a drink at this stone trough,' she says, reminiscing about a time long before main roads and family saloon cars existed.

Eventually, we reach the very top of the hill and arrive at a field which is the enviable home of three miniature ponies and a couple of nonplussed llamas. Mum stops beside the wall and reaches inside her thirty-litre rucksack, moments later pulling out an enormous bag of carrots and three large Granny Smith apples. I can't help wondering how much that rucksack weighed. No wonder she didn't want to tell me what was in it!

'Here you go, sweetheart,' she says to one of the shrunken white ponies with tiny legs no taller than my knee-length boots. It can only just poke its nose over the wall to snuffle a snack from Mum's hand. She tells me that she comes up here most days to give the ponies a few carrots and an apple as a treat. We stand by the wall chatting to each other – and the ponies – and I smile inside, feeling so blooming grateful that my mum is fit and well enough to do this – a tiny, joyful thing. I feel so incredibly grateful that she is … *alive*.

Death. Grief. The loss of a loved one. The death of a parent. These are things that I have mercifully been spared in my life thus far, but they are a universal truth that will catch up with every single one of us – myself included. Perhaps now more than ever before, I am beginning to realise that my parents won't be around forever. As hundreds of thousands of people across the globe mourn the loss of a beloved elderly relative, I realise how lucky I am to be standing here, feeding carrots to a miniature pony over a drystone wall with my mum.

# LISA

Lisa made contact with me following a snowy run I posted on social media at the start of the year – one of those absorbing, joyful runs where you don't realise that you've had a snot icicle hanging from your nose for the last hour … until you see it in full glory on your Instagram running selfie, that is. Her message to me reads:

> Hi Rachel,
> I just read your post and I am 100% in agreement with you! Running has helped me so much over the past year. I've been a casual runner for a while now, but this year it's taken on a whole new meaning for me. I lost my mum in February, so I've been trying to navigate my way through grief and have often felt overwhelmed, completely lost, and at times like giving up. Running has given me a purpose. It gives me space to think and if I feel even a tiny bit better afterwards, it is something for me to hold on to. I've found such a lot of comfort in the running community and by following other people's journeys and reading about their stories.
> Best wishes,
> Lisa

I wanted to speak to Lisa to find out more about her story and to learn how running has helped her to navigate through one of life's most painful rites of passage – the death of a parent.

Her face pops up on the screen and I hardly recognise her – she isn't wearing one of her many luminous running headbands or pairs of crazy, patterned leggings which are so familiar from her social media posts. We all look so different in our non-running daywear, don't we?

I start by asking Lisa about her introduction to running. It all began ten years ago when she and three of her work colleagues decided to enter the Sheffield 10k in an attempt to get fit. Like so many of us, Lisa had never considered herself to be 'sporty' or 'a runner' before, but with the support and encouragement of her colleagues, she managed to complete the 10k event by run/walking. It was by no means a running epiphany. This was the beginning but, sadly, it was also a false start for Lisa. Running disappeared for a long while in the midst of busy life events, careers and travelling. It didn't reappear until six years later when the subject cropped up with some ultrarunning family members over too much Prosecco on New Year's Eve in 2017. The four of them – Lisa, her boyfriend, her sister and her sister's husband – set themselves a goal to run a 10k race in the New Year. This time, Lisa trained properly for the race, and she recalls the distinct feeling of joy and accomplishment after finishing it – something she hadn't experienced those years earlier. It was a turning point of sorts. The seed was sown, and Lisa and her boyfriend decided to set their sights on a half-marathon distance. The makings of the 'Coops Runs' alter ego (Lisa's Instagram handle) was born.

I ask Lisa when running really became a 'thing' for her. Was there a time when she realised that running was something that she needed to do? Does she recall a moment when it dawned on her that running had become such a fundamental part of her life? Her answer is shocking in its simplicity. 'Yes. When my mum died.'

It's not easy to speak about this stuff, let alone to somebody who you've only just met on a Zoom call, but Lisa says that it's actually a relief to be able to talk about it. 'Many people don't know how to talk to me about losing my mum,' she tells me, 'so they tend to avoid the subject completely.' Perhaps this is a typical response to taboo subjects – those we find easier to dodge than to confront head-on. This becomes a discussion point in itself. We chat about how running enables us to talk more openly – to start otherwise difficult conversations that would be easier to avoid. Isn't it funny how you can start a conversation with another runner which can – and often does

– then develop into exploring other, braver topics? Perhaps that's one of the ways running works its magic – enabling us to bond initially over one thing: a love we share; this thing we both understand that helps us in some indescribable way. Somehow, it makes the harder, more challenging conversations easier to tackle. It takes the fear away from what would otherwise be sensitive subjects – including honest discussions around death, grief and loss. It feels like this is exactly what has happened with me and Lisa during the first few minutes of our call. Initially, we began talking about running, and this has laid the groundwork for the heavier stuff. It has already bonded us sufficiently to brave the sensitive topic which is the reason for our conversation today: the experience of Lisa losing her beloved mum, Lil.

Lisa begins to tell me her story. Following a wonderful holiday in September 2019, the family had made plans to meet up in early December. As the date grew closer, Lisa's mum cancelled. It was most unlike her, but she'd been feeling poorly for a while with worsening flu-like symptoms and she was eventually taken into hospital for assessments. Just one week before Christmas, Lil was diagnosed with leukaemia – a cancer of the blood. I hear Lisa say those words and my heart suddenly feels heavy like a stone. The weight of her sadness is palpable; the devastation is visible. This was only a year ago, and I can hear in Lisa's voice the trauma of discovering that her dearest mum was so incredibly poorly. That's bad enough, but the following day, Lisa's gran – her mum's mum – died.

I need to take a breath. I look up from my monitor and I can see a patchwork of fields from my office window. I tell Lisa that I can see open space, green grass, the rolling hills and the most beautiful blue sky. I don't know how to respond to what she has just told me, but as I look outside and take a deep breath, it helps somehow. How does a young woman cope with the devastating diagnosis of a parent followed immediately by the death of a grandparent, and having to deliver the news to her sick mother in a hospital bed?

Lisa smiles as I describe the calming view outside my window and she says, 'It's true, even just looking outside at nature helps. It's like a reminder of life.' In that moment, the heaviness is lifted. 'Being out amongst nature reminds me that there is so much beauty and life out there,' she continues.

I know exactly what she means.

But even this part of Lisa's journey was riddled with challenges. Her solace in running was hampered by an injury she'd sustained while running with her boyfriend in late 2019 – right at the time of her mum's diagnosis. While Lisa was injured, she would go down to the local gym and thrash out her terror and frustrations on the static bike and anything else she could do which didn't aggravate her running injury. She says that she felt compelled to move, she had to do something to vent her inner turmoil, but the one thing she needed more than anything else – running – was simply not an option.

I wonder at Lisa's resilience in the face of all this insurmountable horror, and the grim reality that even her own body was letting her down right at the very time when she needed it the most. Just when running was the biggest tool in her survival kit – when it had become a fundamental part of Lisa's DNA – it disappeared without trace. I can't help but struggle to imagine how she coped. My mind whirs with questions. How did she find the strength to do the things she needed to do every single day? How did the stress not send her spinning into a mental health oblivion like a ten-pin skittle in a bowling alley? There are so many questions, I don't know where to begin.

Lisa was fortunate in that her employer allowed her to take some time off work during this awful period. Normal life was simply put on hold. Her days were filled with endless commutes from London, as the priority was for her to spend as much time as possible with her mum, who was confined to a hospital ward in Sheffield.

While Lil was receiving treatment in hospital, Lisa would frequently send her pictures of herself wearing multicoloured, funky leggings for her workouts in the gym. 'Mum absolutely loved my crazy leggings,' Lisa tells me. 'I used to say to her, "Look! I'm sending you some pedal power, Mum!" It made her smile.' Now it makes sense why the technicolour running tights and headbands are such a prominent feature of Lisa's social media posts – they were for her mum: to will her to recover – like that is even a matter of will – and to make her smile.

Lil was undergoing intensive chemotherapy treatment at the time, which Lisa describes as being 'hellish' – a poison being pumped through Lil's entire system with the intention of eradicating the cancerous cells in her blood. It had a devastating impact on the rest of Lil's body, ultimately resulting in her being admitted to an intensive care ward. As horrendous as this must have been for Lisa's mum to endure, it was also traumatic for the rest of her family, who had no idea how much damage the chemotherapy itself would cause. Despite the torment of seeing Lil so poorly, there were signs that she was becoming stronger. Mercifully, Lisa and her family were given some glimmers of hope. Although the family had no idea what the future might look like, given the punishing impact of the toxic treatment on Lil's frail body, the early indications were good. The family were told that a full recovery was still possible. 'We had hope,' Lisa says wistfully, 'and without that, then what do you have left?'

In fact, the good news didn't end there. Lisa's running injury was also showing signs of improvement and she was starting to run again, albeit tentatively. She began by testing her legs with a few short, steady jogs on the treadmill. To her immense joy, her body responded well, and this was a turning point for running to come back into her life. 'The sheer joy I felt from just being able to run for half a kilometre on the treadmill was indescribable,' Lisa tells me, her eyes lighting up as though she is describing being reunited with a long-lost friend. I can see how much running meant to her; I can hear how much she had missed it throughout the horror of those months and how desperate she was for it to return. Patience, together with some intensive physiotherapy and cross-training, had allowed Lisa's body to gradually recover from her injury.

On her birthday at the start of the year, Lisa went running with her sister and she describes that seven-kilometre run as 'the best birthday present ever'. As usual, she wore her brightly coloured leggings, and she recalls the truly joyful feeling of running returning. 'When you're stuck inside the hospital room, there is nothing but the sterile walls and the gut-wrenching medical information you've been given by people in white coats,' she says. 'For me, being outside and running freely in nature is the antidote to all that.'

Lisa describes sitting in the hospital room with her mum one day when a feeling of complete helplessness engulfed her. 'I realised that I couldn't control anything,' she says. 'I couldn't control my mum's illness; I couldn't control any aspect of her treatment and I couldn't control the outcome. I couldn't control anything at all. It was terrifying.' Sitting beside Lil's hospital bed with her dad and sister, Lisa had the idea of running the Manchester Marathon for a cancer charity. In her words, she felt 'compelled to make something good come out of it'. She talked to her mum, who was thrilled at the idea. 'It gave Mum something positive to focus on,' Lisa says. 'Something away from the illness and the treatment, the hospital wards and beige walls.' And so, a new running challenge was born. Lisa and her boyfriend, together with her sister and brother-in-law, would run the Manchester Marathon for charity. Word spread and more friends wanted to join in and be a part of the enormous swell of positivity arising from an otherwise bleak landscape. They called themselves 'Lil's Army'.

T-shirts were printed with LIL'S ARMY emblazoned in bold across the back, a JustGiving page was set up, and Lil set about telling the doctors and medical staff about her daughter Lisa and the Manchester Marathon which the group of family and friends would be running in April. 'She was so excited,' Lisa says, beaming. They often chatted about it. 'Maybe your dad could drive up to support you?' Lil had suggested, overwhelmed at the prospect that so many people – including those whom she had never even met – were going to run the marathon with her in mind and for a cause so deeply felt by the entire family.

'We all started to believe that things would get better,' Lisa says.

Having survived the onslaught of the chemotherapy treatment, plans were made for Lil to return home. Lisa recalls speaking to her mum on the phone at the beginning of February, by which time she had already been in hospital for the best part of two months. 'She sounded like my mum again,' Lisa says, recollecting that conversation just before her mum was due to be discharged – something the family had been praying for ever since the devastating diagnosis months earlier.

But Lisa's mum wouldn't be returning home. Just two days later, Lisa received a telephone call in the early hours of a Sunday morning. On hearing her dad's voice, she sensed it was bad news. Lil had fallen during the night and banged her head, suffering a catastrophic bleed on the brain. Tragically, in her weakened state, Lil fell into a coma. Lisa caught the first train out of London knowing that she was going to see her mum for one last time. She sat with Lil for the following twenty-four hours. 'When it came, it was peaceful,' she tells me. 'At least we got to say goodbye.'

Here I go, looking out of the window again. My heart is breaking for Lisa – this lovely young woman with tears in her eyes and a heart torn apart. She asks me: 'How does a person process that?' I don't know, I tell her. I simply have no idea. I wish I could reach through the monitor and give Lisa a hug. I wish I could be there next to her and hold her hand as she tells me this story. I can feel her pain. I want to say something to comfort her, but I have no idea what words to choose. What happened seems so cruel and so utterly devastating that I cannot imagine putting myself in Lisa's shoes. People use the word 'overwhelm', and in the purest sense, this is simply and entirely overwhelming – as though it could knock a person over without any chance of them knowing how to get back up.

I'm trying to be professional here. I can't start bawling into my computer screen. Lisa is immensely brave. She is talking openly with me – a complete stranger other than through our virtual worlds of social media – about a subject which might ordinarily feel almost impossible. Lisa (who also happens to be a qualified counsellor) says that she knows about the benefits of talking. 'Loss and bereavement still feel to be such taboo subjects in society, and I truly believe that they need to be talked about more openly. When I look back on what happened, I don't honestly know how I got through it,' she says. 'But the fact is, we *do* get through these things, as hideous as they are at the time.'

Lisa tells me that she still breaks down from time to time; she still has difficulty working and concentrating on occasion. She says that her mum was her best friend. I have one of those shocking being-slapped-across-the-face moments. I think about my daughter and about my mum. I think about my relationship with them both. I think about holding my little girl's soft, silky hands, and my mum's bony, protruding knuckles and her paper-thin, translucent skin. This isn't some distant, abstract story. It feels so painfully close. Those of us who have any kind of mother–daughter relationship can surely feel Lisa's story lapping up on our own shores.

And then, just as the family were in the depth of their grief, the Covid-19 pandemic took hold and the Manchester Marathon was cancelled. 'It became even more important for us to run,' Lisa says, explaining how – despite the worst of all realities – the objective of Lil's Army running the marathon was a lifeline at a time of personal crisis. 'It gave us something positive to focus on,' she says. 'It was a goal – something we could do together – and something my mum had been so excited about, which meant everything to her ... and to us.'

With Covid changing every aspect of life, it was unfeasible for Lil's Army to run the Manchester Marathon as they had planned, but they weren't defeated. They ran a socially distanced relay marathon instead. Lisa ran 10k from her home, returned and handed over to her boyfriend, who did the same. One by one, they called the next person to let them know: 'Right – off you go. It's your turn ... '

The goal of running a marathon stopped Lisa from being swept away by grief and loss at a time when she could so easily have succumbed to her overwhelming sadness. It was a branch she could hold on to, a temporary reprieve from being completely engulfed by heartbreak and injustice. It was a way of physically working through her shock and grief as though it needed to be released from her body in some way, freeing it – if only momentarily – from her mind.

As Lisa has been telling me her story, I feel like Buddy from *Elf* as he runs round and round in a department store's revolving door and then staggers across the road and throws up in a bin. One shock to deal with on top of another. Her family have endured so much. They have had their lives turned completely upside down; they have lost the one person in the world who they loved the most. To add to this, the entire globe has been ambushed by a deadly virus and – right at the start of the Covid pandemic – the family set up a small army of supporters who ran a socially distanced marathon raising vital funds for charity ... all within the space of a year. It is quite staggering. Planning to run a marathon and training for it is one thing; dealing with injury and recovery is another – that would be more than enough for most of us to cope with at any one time – but Lisa had significantly more on her plate.

Lil knew how much Lisa loved running. She was aware how much the marathon goal meant to her, and she knew the power it had in keeping her focused on positivity and giving her a purpose which was bigger than the terror she was experiencing. I ask Lisa if she was surviving on pure adrenaline at the time, simply keeping going because the alternative – stillness – was too terrifying for her to comprehend. 'I wasn't even aware of what I was doing at the time,' she tells me. 'I just needed to get my trainers on, go outside and run. I'm not sure that conscious thought was even a part of it.'

Lisa explains that she wasn't initially fully able to process the reality of the Covid-19 pandemic, which is hardly surprising given that she had lost her mother just a handful of weeks before. I try and put myself in Lisa's position. It must have been difficult enough to process the dreadful and shocking way in which her mother died, let alone to then be thrust into the midst of a global pandemic where all of a sudden familiar places are in lockdown and normal life as we know it has ground to a complete halt. Much has been said about the impact of the pandemic on mental health, but surely managing that *in addition to* the grief that Lisa was already experiencing must have been an almost insurmountable assault on her mental health. 'The impact of the pandemic didn't hit me straight away,' she tells me. 'I simply couldn't deal with it on top of everything else. If I sat still for too long, anxiety and depression would just engulf me. I couldn't think straight – I would just cry.'

There's something about the strength of Lisa's instinct in knowing what would help her cope and survive – perhaps it's our DNA guiding us rather than it being a conscious, calculated thought. But there is no doubt that Lisa was compelled towards physical movement and running as a way of managing her grief and – ultimately – saving her mental health. It's not all heavy talk. We share a laugh at the fact that she has enjoyed doing *PE with Joe Wicks* – the lockdown children's fitness sessions – at 9 a.m. most days throughout lockdown.

I ask Lisa how she believes running has helped her over the last year. 'It has given me a break from the constant sadness and endless crying,' she says, describing running as 'freedom from grief'. She points out that it's far harder to cry when you're running – it's a fair point! To be clear, Lisa isn't in any way suggesting that it's preferable to repress those emotions or to stop yourself from expressing them – it's just that she welcomed the brief periods of reprieve when they came. Like coming up for air.

What is running to Lisa now? I ask her this question and the smile spreads right across her face. She tells me about the ultramarathon that she has completed since her mum died – a distance of thirty-two miles – and her plans to return to the Manchester Marathon in her mum's memory. 'I'm going to run it with my sister,' she tells me. 'It's something that means so much to us both and it's something we can do together.'

I feel like I've found a running kindred spirit in Lisa, and I have no doubt that all the ways in which running has helped her throughout the devastating loss of her mum are the same anchors I would turn to. Not only in helping to manage grief, but in bringing positivity and joy to fill a void created by loss. From Lisa I have learnt that running is a celebration of life as much as it is a way of dealing with death.

Since sharing her story with me, Lisa has run a virtual marathon on the first anniversary of her mum's death. 'I ran fifteen laps of some local fields in the snow, mostly on my own. I had my boyfriend and two friends come to run a couple of laps with me, and a support crew who made me an aid station stocked with energy drinks and Creme Eggs!' Lisa says that this is one of her greatest personal achievements.

She and her boyfriend have since relocated to Sheffield, where they enjoy running together around the Peak District. 'We discovered a loop through picturesque villages, beautiful river valleys and up to the top of the heather-covered peaks. It made me feel alive and excited to have all this on my doorstep.' Since completing her ultramarathon, Lisa believes that this is where she wants to focus her running in the future. 'I enjoy the sense of adventure and the fact that I can stop for a snack! I'm not a fast runner and pushing myself to run faster isn't always enjoyable for me. I like the longer distances.'

# GINA

It's the beginning of our call and I'm immediately struck by how vibrant and effervescent Gina is. She reminds me of a springer spaniel I once had called Daisy: full of life and happiest when she was running free and chasing sticks in the woods. I loved her dearly but, honestly, it was harder than having a baby.

'Nowadays, I'm an open person,' Gina tells me. It's interesting that she begins our conversation this way, the inference being that she didn't use to be like this. She has reached out to tell me about how running has helped her to deal with a mental health breakdown caused by stress at work, and to subsequently redesign her life. Wow! I think back to the time when I quit my legal career and retrained as a personal trainer, going on to set up a fitness studio in a converted old chicken shed. I know how it feels to be stuck in a job – and in a life – that doesn't fit. I know how soul-destroying it is to shoehorn yourself into a lifestyle that feels like it's crushing you from the inside out. I'm fascinated to hear Gina's story and to find out how she went from that place to the joyful, energetic person I see in front of me today.

'I'd always wanted to be a teacher,' Gina tells me. 'I loved teaching so much. It was my passion.' She worked hard and progressed quickly through her career, ultimately taking a position as a head teacher – the job she had been striving for from the outset.

Outwardly, Gina's career couldn't have been going any better – she had achieved the very thing she had set her heart on. But inside, she was suffering badly with impostor syndrome. I'm sure you know the feeling

– I certainly do. The one where you are constantly waiting to be 'found out' – for somebody to discover that you can't do it (whatever the 'it' is for you) – and realise that you are, in fact, a fraud. Side note: I was awarded an honorary degree in 2020 for my 'significant personal achievement and contribution to the discussion around mental health'. Guess what my acceptance speech was about? Impostor syndrome. Like Gina, I know the feeling well.

'I would sit in meetings and constantly compare myself to other people,' Gina says. 'I would tell myself to "try and be more like *that* person". It was a complete nightmare.' This way of thinking made her job doubly hard: she was desperately trying to portray the image of a person who was in complete control while self-doubt gnawed away at her from the inside. And this pattern got worse throughout her career. With every new role and increased pressure of management and responsibility, the louder the pangs of insecurity grew.

Following one particularly gruelling Ofsted inspection in 2018, Gina felt the true impact of her self-doubts when she took the damning report on her school's performance to be confirmation that *she* was failing. She was an impostor; she was a fraud. This was the tipping point for Gina, who internalised all the purported failings and 'areas for improvement' to be about her personally, and not about the school. 'It broke me completely,' she says, describing it being 'like living in a permanent, heavy fog'. And that wasn't the only thing that felt wrong in her life; because of the insurmountable stress Gina was living with daily, *everything* did.

At Christmastime, Gina took a step back and discussed her predicament with her husband. 'I was forty-four at the time,' she says. 'I felt afraid of quitting teaching and starting all over again.' I can sense immediately that overcoming the 'age barrier' is something Gina is incredibly passionate about. She went to her GP, who signed her off work with stress – something which caused Gina to panic even more. The fear and the shame of failure – or at least, having failed in her own eyes – lay heavy on Gina's heart.

With her energy and self-esteem at an all-time low, Gina's husband, David, suggested that she should start running again, the mountain of work pressures having left her no time or energy to even contemplate putting her running shoes on for a long while. 'I felt like I'd lost my identity, my career, my self-worth, and I was even afraid of going into my local town for fear of bumping into one of the school parents.'

The impact of Gina's professional life adversely affected her quality of life and that of her family to the extent that she wanted to escape from it completely. 'I'd become frightened of absolutely everything,' she says, knowing without any doubt that something had to change.

I know how she feels. I was twenty-seven years old when I left my legal career behind. It took me all my courage to do that and to deal with the onslaught of disbelieving gasps that I was 'throwing away a perfectly good career' to go and open a gym in a dirty old chicken shed. But then, I didn't have any children; I was seventeen years younger than Gina was when she was faced with the same crossroads, and I remember at the time feeling 'old' (I gasp in horror as I am writing this!). So, how does a forty-four-year-old mum of two make that change? How did Gina go about redesigning her life to make it feel joyful and purposeful again?

Gina started running with a friend. There was no magic formula. They would run together and chat, and it wasn't very long before Gina started to feel different. 'It sounds mad, but running started to build my confidence,' she tells me. 'The more I went out running, I began to realise that ... I CAN DO THIS!' I reassure Gina that what she is saying *doesn't* sound mad. Not in the slightest. 'I was starting to replace the negative thoughts I had about myself with more positive ones. I began to *look forward* to things again – it was a feeling I hadn't had in a long time.' Like turning around a huge ocean tanker, over the following months Gina's head finally started to believe in the words 'YOU CAN ... !' She started to believe in herself again.

Gina's close friends soon began to notice the changes, making comments such as, 'Finally! Thank God you're back!' Gina fully credits running with her transformation, going from a listless person who simply wanted to hide herself away to a woman filled with energy who loved life again. And it came at just the right time. Gina was at a crossroads in her life. Would she go back to the high-pressured job and the career progression that was – in her words – killing her? Or would she make a different choice?

I think it's important to note here that changing jobs and shifting to another career is a complex and challenging decision to make. Gina's decision was fraught with worry and uncertainty. Nobody turns their back on years of hard study or career progression on a whim; few people have the freedom to change tack like that without a huge impact on every other aspect of their lives. What about income? How do you pay the bills? If you need to take time out for retraining or further education, what happens then? How do you survive? Gina had been financially independent all her adult life. She had never relied on anybody else to prop her up financially or in any other way. But this time, she knew that she needed to reframe the parameters of her relationship and allow her husband to support her while she went through the metamorphosis into a happier life. 'It scared me to even think about going back into that stressful, toxic life,' Gina tells me. And so, with the full backing and encouragement of her family, she strode forward into the unknown. She knew that her mental health depended on it, and she believed strongly – as I did – in the long-term reward of being brave and making such a decision when the alternative was quite simply unthinkable.

One of the effects of Gina's dramatic turnaround was her realisation that she wanted to redesign her life and help other people benefit in the same way. 'Running was helping me to discover myself again,' she says, 'and I knew then that I wanted to help other people do that for themselves.' One of Gina's proudest running achievements was when she led a group of ten ladies with absolutely no running experience to complete their first ever 5k. 'For eight weeks we met every week; we ran, we walked, we talked and we supported each other,' she tells me. 'The thought of it still makes me emotional! It wasn't just the fact that we achieved our goal, it was about the journey that we all went on. Yes, we had the odd tough week, but we never gave up, and by the end they saw themselves as runners. The negative self-talk was now a thing of the past!'

I'm conscious that throughout this book I describe many 'Me too!' moments – those where I can strongly relate to an aspect of another person's story. I'm almost at the point of disbelieving the number of synergies myself, but here comes another one. At the point of leaving my legal career, I too felt strongly that I wanted to help empower other people – especially women

– to become physically and mentally stronger and more confident, as I had done by gradually working on my fitness and taking a firm grip of my mental health struggles. In hindsight, my motivation in helping to empower others to make positive changes in their lives was the same as Gina's.

It is no exaggeration to say that running enabled Gina to believe in a completely new trajectory for her life. It was running that allowed her to build the blocks of self-belief and it was running that brought a clarity and a calm to her mind which had been absent for so long. How is that possible? How does running help people like myself and Gina believe that they have other choices, and consider that there is an alternative to the path they are on, especially when pressure to return to toxic careers is all around? 'Everybody expected me to go back to my old job,' she says. I know how she felt – it's like being a fish and swimming upstream. *'YOU'RE GOING THE WRONG WAY!'* But Gina wasn't going the wrong way; she was following all the signs that were *screaming* at her to change direction. That is incredibly hard to do in the face of endless doubt and scepticism. Gina likens her choice to being in a destructive relationship. 'It's easier to go back into a toxic relationship, even when you know it's damaging for you, just because you're scared of the unknown.' We chat about it further and I wonder whether running acts as a bridge to get us to the other side of the gaping void. Is running the thing that enables us to contemplate the future we can't see, and yet we believe is out there? Does running give us the strength to stare into the face of uncertainty, instead of deepening the grooves which would otherwise have us trapped in a life that we know is wrong for us? Does running allow us to believe that there is something better waiting for us on the other side? Not in the sense that the grass will be greener (it never is), but that other alternatives might be *possible*?

Gina describes the way that running has helped her to discover her 'authentic self' again. I don't know if Oprah has the legal right to such phrases, which admittedly make me wince a little. Discovering the real you means getting to know the deeper parts of yourself and growing to like – and even to love – that person. No longer hiding behind a persona, as Gina was doing while in her head teacher role. That wasn't the real Gina. It was a highly stressed, deeply unhappy version of the *real* person who was lost underneath layers of social conditioning. The real Gina was discovered again while out on runs by herself and with friends where the most natural version of the person everybody knew as 'Gina' could be seen in her most joyful state. We wear masks every single day. We act in a certain way while we're at work; we make efforts to portray a certain image while waiting for our children outside the school gates. It is relentless. When are we in our most natural state? When does the façade come down? For many of us, the answer is that, sadly, it never does. It doesn't get to come down because we have forgotten who we are. We have lost the ability to see ourselves other than in the various roles we play with whatever stresses are attached. Running is arguably one of the few places where we can take off the veneer and just be. That is Gina's experience and it is my own.

At times during our call, Gina tries to explain what happened to make the seismic shift in her life and she looks genuinely puzzled, as though she barely understands any of it herself. I can relate to this, too. It is at times impossible to articulate how running frees the mind: it's too big, too all-consuming. After a few moments, the words finally come. 'I stopped being afraid,' she tells me. Along with building her self-belief, running made Gina feel safe. Isn't that incredible?

It strikes me that Gina embodies so much of the 'good stuff' about running. She is effervescent and sparky; she is animated and colourful. She is the personification of the joys of running. It makes me wonder about the possibility that those of us – like Gina – who have discovered the magic of running almost carry that around with us, emitting positive rays out into the universe. We often talk about people being weighed down when referring to life struggles of various kinds, giving an image of them dragging along a heavy ball and chain. What about the opposite being the case? Is it possible that somebody could carry with them the joys of running and exude self-belief and possibility, like a brightness that others can see and feel? Speaking to Gina, I believe that it is.

During my many conversations with people throughout the process of writing this book, various phrases have been used and endless analogies given to the transformation brought about by running. 'It's like I was reborn,' Martin told me, describing the person who emerged on the other side of binge drinking and failed relationships. From talking to people like Gina and Martin I wonder if, rather than becoming 'a new person' through running, we are instead going back to discover the oldest parts of ourselves – the people who existed before the social pressures and work anxiety, before peer pressure and modern-day trappings. Perhaps that's it. Maybe running helps us to discover who we were all along.

Gina says that she wouldn't change any aspect of her experience – even the awful parts. 'Having been at rock bottom, I have something to compare how my life is now,' she tells me. Gina feels a particular affinity with women who think it's too late for them to make a life change. She's talking about women in their forties and beyond who may feel as though the time has been and gone for them to make sweeping changes such as quitting a toxic relationship or an unfulfilling career. 'I'm passionate about getting the message across to other people that changing your life is possible,' she says. Gina wants other women to know that there is more to life; there are options for making change even when it feels 'too late' or hopeless. It isn't. And Gina is living, breathing proof of the fact.

I ask Gina how she feels now. 'My life is incredible,' she says. She spends her days encouraging others to be fit and healthy and teaching them how to build up their own self-esteem. 'All my skills are transferable,' she tells me. 'I can still teach, but doing it this way has absolutely transformed my life.' I seriously doubt whether it would be possible for Gina to be any happier. By the end of the call, I only wish I lived closer so that I could attend one of her fitness classes.

Since sharing her story with me, Gina has continued running with her own ladies' fitness community. 'My experience has taught me that without self-belief, life is a struggle. Running has helped to lift me out of a very dark place. I want to use my fitness classes/running groups to teach women the importance of exercise – we are not punishing our bodies; we are celebrating them!' Gina has also committed to pushing her own limits by entering into a half-Ironman event later in the year. 'My "I can't" has turned into "I can!" and even if I don't quite get there, I will always enjoy the journey.'

# LARS-CHRISTIAN

A message pings into my inbox. It's short and sweet. Quite unremarkable, really.

> Hey, Rachel.
> I thought you might be interested in the running newsletter I send out every Monday. It's a very simple concept: to inspire people with a run workout, a picture and a quote. I think you might like it.
> Thanks for taking a look.
> Lars-Christian

A newsletter about running? Sounds simple enough. Sure! I'm happy to take a look.

I click on the web link and expect to see exactly what Lars has described – a run workout, a picture and an inspiring quote. But then I dig a little deeper and I stumble across Lars's reason for starting to run in the first place and for writing his newsletter. What I discover is so much more than I had anticipated.

> I took up running to improve my physical and mental wellbeing and to help me deal with the loss of my daughter …

Those five words spin around in my head. *The loss of my daughter …* They stop me in my tracks.

We're here again – where running appears at a place of utter devastation.

Lars and I exchange a few messages and we arrange to speak on a Zoom call. I feel understandably apprehensive about this one. How does a person talk openly about the loss of a child to a complete stranger? It's one thing losing a parent, and although grief can't be classified into relative sub-categories, I honestly can't imagine a more devastating grief than the loss of a child – the end of a life yet to be lived.

I need to make absolutely sure that Lars is happy to talk to me about his experience. When I put my concerns to him, I receive this reply.

*Hi Rachel.*

*I want to talk about what I've been through because I truly believe that running can change a person's life. It is why I do what I do with my Run161 newsletter. I simply want to help people discover and embrace running, and to truly experience its healing power. I'm happy to share my story because I believe that it can offer comfort, solace and even hope to someone who might need it – just like I did. And, by extension, it means that my little girl continues to make the world a better place – as short as her life may have been.*

Lars explains that 'Run161' is a representation of his daughter's name, Iben. You see, she is everywhere. She is at the very heart of Lars's running. She is in every single mile he runs and in the places that nobody else can see.

In the front of my first book, *Running for My Life*, I wrote a dedication for my daughter. It says, 'To my beautiful Tilly. Thank you for being my reason why.' My daughter was the reason for setting myself the goal to take control of my physical and mental health. Lars's daughter, Iben, is the reason for his discovery of running and for wanting to share its incredible healing powers with the world. Although for very different reasons, our daughters have propelled us both towards running. It has saved us both in some way.

The day arrives and it's time for our call. The truth is, I can't honestly think what I'm going to say, but I decide to be open about it rather than try to pretend otherwise. Lars explains that even before his daughter was conceived, he had experienced some mental health struggles. He tells me that he had difficulty finding meaning and purpose in his life and he had experienced troubling, intrusive thoughts right through adolescence and into early adulthood. 'Things have been very dark at times,' he says.

Like many little boys, Lars grew up playing football. He was a talented youngster and had hopes of playing professionally at some level. But when that didn't happen in his early twenties, he gave it up and desperately hoped that something else would fill the void that playing football had left in his life. It didn't work out that way, and depression set in. Lars explains that throughout those years, the lost, hopeless feelings began to take a firm hold. It was then that the search began – a search to fill the void that he felt so strongly, a sense that there was something missing in his life.

'People talk about finding meaning or purpose in life, and having a child can appear to be an answer to that void. When my wife became pregnant with our daughter in late 2016, a large part of me hoped that becoming a parent would fill the emptiness that I'd been feeling for so long. I started thinking of my unborn daughter as the person who was going to save me in some way.'

To prepare himself for fatherhood, Lars began running during his wife's pregnancy. He talks about the ways in which he was fearful that his daughter would grow up experiencing the same kind of sadness and depression, perhaps even feeling unsure of her own place in the world. Lars wrangled with these troubled thoughts throughout his wife's pregnancy. Running helped him when his mind would jump to an indeterminate time in the future – a time when his unborn daughter would be a young girl facing her own challenges growing up. Lars's first instinct was to look ahead and try to work out how to help his little girl avoid making the same mistakes. Running helped him to process the many anxieties and the anticipation of becoming a father, preparing him for adversity even before his daughter was born.

But things took a devastating turn. In early June 2017, Lars's life would change forever when Iben was delivered early by emergency caesarean section. For five torturous days following the premature birth, Lars and his wife waited to see if there were any signs that their daughter would survive. On the fifth day, they were told that she would not recover, having suffered significant brain damage as a result of receiving too little oxygen in the womb.

It is truly horrific to hear a story like this. How can anyone who hasn't experienced that kind of complete devastation come anywhere close to knowing how it feels? There are no words I can find – I will never know what that pain is like. It is simply inconceivable.

Lars explains the precise moment when running appeared to him, right in the midst of his tsunami of grief. His parents had arrived from the other side of the country, and while travelling in the car with his parents, his mother turned to Lars and asked him, 'Do you think you'll continue running?'

'No,' he replied, feeling as though he simply had no reason to continue running – or doing anything else in particular.

But Lars realised in that moment he'd just used his daughter's death as a reason to *not* do something he loved which was so good for him. He decided that he couldn't let his daughter be a reason to stop doing the one thing that he needed so much in his life.

'I realised straight away that my initial answer was wrong. It wasn't what my heart was telling me,' he says. Lars knew then that he would turn the memory of his daughter and her six short days of life into something meaningful – a force to propel him forwards even in the depth of his grief and despair. He was determined to make something positive come from the loss of his little girl. Right at the very moment he told his mother that he wouldn't continue running, he knew that his answer had already changed.

From there, Lars set himself a goal to run a sub-three-hour marathon. For anyone who knows a thing or two about marathon running, this is the kind of marathon time that few non-elite runners even dream of, let alone achieve. Lars describes it as being a 'ridiculous goal' because he honestly didn't believe that he had any chance of realising it, but he decided that this was his plan anyway. I ask him to put his goal into context. What kind of runner was he at the time? Lars tells me that he was a forty-five-minute 10k runner at this point in his life, and he had barely any experience of running races. The only thing in his favour was his athletic background of football training, which he believes gave him a good basic level of fitness.

Following the loss of his daughter, Lars tells me that days lost their meaning. There was precious little difference between day and night. Nothing seemed to make any sense or have any purpose. Lars and his wife made a commitment to each other to spend some time outside each day. They both knew that this would heal them in different ways. Lars would run when he could, and they would support each other in doing the things they needed to do to be okay, day after day.

And so, he ran. For the first month, Lars describes how his body was decimated with grief. Physically, he was completely shattered – torn apart. 'I struggled to run a single kilometre,' he tells me. His heart rate was sky-high even while running slowly – and so any lofty marathon goals were out of the question. He mentions something he gleaned from Haruki Murakami's book *What I Talk About When I Talk About Running*: 'Running doesn't fix anything; but it pauses everything.' Running gave Lars some respite from the physical experience of grief which was so all-consuming and relentless. Running – however pained and however slowly – allowed him a brief reprieve from his sorrow.

Lars had to crawl through the grief by putting his trainers on every day before he could even contemplate the training required to be able to achieve his sub-three-hour marathon goal. I ask how he went from barely being able to shuffle one foot in front of the other to training seriously for a fast marathon. Some of his best friends had noticed that he had started running. They made contact and encouraged him to run a half marathon with them. It was a goal that would bring them together (they were located in different parts of the country), and by uniting with a common focus, they could share in each other's journeys and support each other along the way. If nothing else, the group of friends would spend a fun weekend together with a half marathon thrown in for good measure! This was a few months after losing Iben, and Lars explains that setting this half-marathon goal gave him a sense of purpose, and he believes it was the catalyst he needed for his competitive spark to return. It required him to look into training more seriously and it helped him to take a step forward through his grief. 'Talking with my best friends helped,' he says. Community and friendship together with a clear focus made all the difference. I ask Lars how this enabled him to deal with his grief. 'The truth is, you don't move on from the grief,' he says. 'You just learn to grow with it.' Lars describes his experience of grieving as being something that is at first simply too heavy to carry. 'You start off feeling so incredibly weak,' he says. 'But then you become stronger. Slowly, you grow with it, and you learn how to carry the weight. But it never goes away.'

As somebody who has never had to face this kind of loss, I find Lars's explanation extremely helpful in understanding how grief feels. To learn that it doesn't go away, to hear that you don't 'leave your grief behind' or 'just come out of it' is incredibly insightful for somebody who has yet to experience this in her lifetime. And to liken the grieving process to becoming stronger and more able to bear the weight of the loss makes sense to me, too. Perhaps just as running strengthens our muscles and tendons and increases our aerobic capacity, it also helps to toughen those parts of our character that we need in order to deal with trauma and adversity. Lars describes coping with his grief being like building endurance: 'Once you begin to feel that you can learn to live with the grief – that you can tolerate it – then you realise that nothing else can hurt you in life.' He says, 'If you can survive this, then you can survive anything.'

Lars kept on running and training for the half marathon, but in the back of his mind, he was already in training for the sub-three-hour marathon which he had promised Iben that he would do everything in his power to achieve.

Lars completed the half-marathon race. Afterwards, he and his wife went away on a holiday. While on that vacation, he had another epiphany. He realised that he wasn't just training because he had a goal to complete – he was doing it because he loved running. He understood that running fed his soul, and he hadn't experienced a feeling like that since his days of playing football. The dawning of just how much passion he had for running and how much he wanted it to be a part of his life smacked Lars between the eyes. He instantly connected this feeling with his daughter, and he says it felt like he'd received a special gift from her. Lars describes the sense of receiving the gift of running from Iben and it filling a void which he had felt in his life for so long. The search was over – he was certain that this gift had come from his little girl. He knew in that moment that he would never stop running.

Our experiences are polar opposites, but we both share the same experience of realising on a very deep level how much running means to us. We talk about the enormity of this – the fact that we both *need* running in our lives. It fills a part of us that nothing else can. For me, it symbolises my life truly beginning after decades of mental health struggles; for Lars, it is his reason to carry on.

I ask Lars how he took this gift of running forward in his life. He tells me that once he becomes passionate about something, he throws himself into it wholeheartedly. He is an 'all or nothing' kind of guy. The moments of pure joy Lars experienced while out running meant that he committed to doing all he could to treasure running and use it as a force for good in his life. He read every running book, joined every online running community and talked about running with anyone who would listen. Lars immersed himself fully into every conceivable aspect of running. He learnt all he could about training methods and began to scale up his training as quickly as his body adapted. He was soon training six days and running 100 kilometres per week.

The next part of Lars's story is about his desire to share his learning with others. He explains that for him, learning only really makes sense when you are able to connect with others, pass on that knowledge and exchange ideas. Sharing is a natural part of the learning process. Lars believes that his openness and willingness to share his ideas, thoughts and learning around running helped him to do the same with his grief. 'Being open about the grief and learning to talk about it helped me and my wife to keep the memory of Iben alive – to talk about her and to keep her a part of our lives whilst also dealing with our own sense of loss.'

Lars decided to use the gift he had been given – the discovery of his deep love of running – and pass it on to other people. 'That is Iben's legacy,' he says. 'It means that her impact on the world – however short – was a good one.'

'I had to write it all down,' he tells me. Here is the very first blog post Lars wrote, entitled 'Father's Day Run':

*The ice is crushing and crunching under my feet as my spiked winter running shoes keep me glued to the ground. They don't offer the most comfortable run, but compared to the alternative of wearing a helmet to protect me from the outcome of running in slippery conditions like these, the spikes win out by a margin.*

*The calendar shows it is 12 November 2017, and in Norway, it's Father's Day. The first since I became a father. The day also marks five months and a day since my little girl was born.*

*Ice crunches under my feet and I slip a bit on the uneven surface. I manage to keep my balance – no harm done – and I stride on, thinking about that day, five months and one day ago.*

*I ran on that day, and the run lasted a little over an hour and thirty-eight minutes. It wasn't a race, but it's not something you quickly forget, on the day your first child was born. Of lesser significance is the fact that it was the first time I ran the half-marathon distance in under an hour and forty minutes, which was the goal I set for myself at the start of the year. 'What times can I post in my race in September?' I thought, after completing the run on the day my daughter was born.*

*After that, I didn't think about running for a while. My daughter was born on a Sunday – a month before we expected her arrival – and the next Saturday she left this world again whilst in our arms.*

*The ice continues to crack beneath my feet, and I feel tired, but I'm not tired from running. It is Father's Day today, and I'm thinking about my little girl as I look towards the sun which is sitting high in the perfectly blue sky.*

*It wasn't supposed to end up like this, but what can you do? I don't know, so I just run.*

*About halfway through the run, I stop to take a gel. While the temperature is hovering around freezing point, the back of my jacket is saturated from sweat underneath the vest I'm wearing to bring along my water, phone and gel. My stomach has been a challenge through many runs, but as I am going to complete a marathon at some point in the near future, I need to practise nutrition while running.*

*On the day the doctors informed us that there was nothing they could do for our little girl, my mother asked me if I would continue to run after all this had come to an end. We were driving home from the hospital for a quick shower and a change of clothes before going back to spend the night with our daughter, Iben. I remember that the question stumped me at first. At that point, I couldn't imagine ever again having the energy to run, and so I answered 'No'.*

*The gel is supposed to taste like a combination of strawberry and banana, and to my surprise it's not too bad. I drink some water to wash down as much of it as possible before putting my gloves back on and picking up the pace again. The sun has melted away most of the ice from the sidewalk, and the feeling of my spikes on asphalt sends shivers up through my feet and into the rest of my body.*

*When the thought first struck me of not continuing running, I felt guilty for the answer I had given my mom. How could I possibly even contemplate letting my little girl's short life be an excuse for not accomplishing something I'd said I would do? Everything I did and continue to do from the day I first got to hold her has been and will be for her. But this – this one thing that I had somehow thought I wouldn't do because of her – became something I had to do for her. So now I train for the marathon because I have to do it. I have to do it for her.*

*These hills feel like hard work, and the combination of ice and spikes is making my legs feel heavy as I come up to the cemetery where we laid our baby girl to rest just a few months ago. 'I'll see you in a bit, little one,' I whisper as I turn around and run away from the graveyard.*

*It is my first Father's Day, and I have spent it lighting a candle at my daughter's grave.*

*It wasn't supposed to turn out this way, but what can you do? I don't know, and so I just run.*

*Just a couple of miles to go, and the sun has risen completely now. I'm sweating and I try to stay hydrated by practising doing two things at once – drinking and running at the same time.*

*It feels like all days are hard at the moment, and it has been a particularly unsettling week. You get used to feeling down, sad and despondent, but this week everything has felt crooked – a little out of place. Going for a long run in the pouring rain felt like the last thing I wanted to do, but what else was I going to do? So, I ran, of course.*

*A short climb and downhill to go before today's session is over. The wind is cold and gentle, and it is blowing on my face, cooling my entire body which is warm from running. Ask me to describe the perfect day, and I will answer something like this: 'The world is bright white and covered in snow, the sun is shining in the blue sky, and I am outside – right there in the middle of it. Running, skiing or sledging: it doesn't matter, as long as my cheeks are red by the time I get inside to warm up again.'*

*On my run a few days ago, a car splashed me, and I was soaked through to the bone. As the rain turned to sleet, the temperature sank, and the wind picked up and it went from cold to freezing. Running is usually a break from feeling anything much at all, but then I found myself not just freezing, but feeling as physically and mentally broken as I have done for almost five months. 'I can't take this,' I thought, 'I can't go on unless someone saves me.'*

*On the final downhill, as I approach our house, I can see across the fields and the top of the church tower where my little girl rests. As I let my feet go, my shoes still keeping me glued to the road, I think about what a great day this was for a run. A layer of snow covers the world around me, and my cheeks are red as I'm finishing up the final hundred metres or so. I needed saving, and someone gave me a perfect day.*

*It's Father's Day, and it was never meant to be like this. But I know that someone's looking out for me while I run.*

Lars continues to share his passion for running through his Run161 newsletter but explains that it is constantly evolving. 'I don't have a fixed idea in my head about how this should work,' he tells me. 'I don't have a plan. It's just a thing I do.'

He is simply following the path as it appears in front of him, like Hansel and Gretel following the trail of breadcrumbs. I can only imagine that there is something we can all take from this: the ability to not look too far ahead, but to tackle what is right in front of us, one step at a time. Perhaps this is how Lars is able to deal with his grief – taking one day and then the next by following the breadcrumbs. And perhaps running has taught him how to do this; learning how to live in the moment.

Surely Lars's gift to the rest of us is in him sharing his journey and his passion for running and keeping his daughter's memory alive.

Since sharing his story with me, Lars tells me that he has recently been proud to see his wife start her own journey with running just two months after giving birth to their third child. He also tells me that the past few months have been challenging for his own running. 'My body has, for whatever reason, not wanted to train and race at the level I have become used to,' he says. Lars has instead been forced to replace chasing his personal best times with balancing his ambition in an attempt to be able to train consistently again. 'What this period has taught me, however, is that the most important aspect of running is not racing or "running fast". It is simply getting outside, moving, enjoying time in nature and making space for thought and reflection. To breathe fresh air.'

# HANNAH

I have an appointment to see a consultant spinal surgeon later this week. The pain in my lumbar spine has been getting progressively worse and I am now in a place where I never imagined I would ever be: suffering from chronic pain whilst trying to manage as best I can to live the active lifestyle that has propped up my mental health for so long. I'm way past the point of feeling teary-eyed that this year's London Marathon is a write-off for me; I am somewhere else completely. I am now managing my daily pain with medication whilst religiously completing my physiotherapy exercises in the vain hope that I can sit down and walk around without being in permanent discomfort.

Up to this episode I have never really considered what it might be like to live with a chronic condition – one where there is no particular end in sight, just the rumbling on of some issue which requires ongoing medical attention or limits daily activities, or both. I have been incredibly fortunate. I've had many years of immeasurably good health and despite over a decade on mental health medication, in the eleven years since, I have been physically and mentally fitter than many. But now something has changed and it's time for me to find out (for I don't yet know how long) what it is like to have to live with a chronic condition – one which requires pain management and lifestyle moderation every single day.

But this is a reality for millions of people. I'm not alone. For all I know (and I don't know very much just yet), I might be one of the lucky ones. There might be some end in sight for me, whereas others sadly have no such prospect.

It makes me wonder – what is it like for a person in chronic pain who wants to live an active lifestyle?

Hannah has a history of endometriosis, a particularly painful condition whereby tissue similar to the womb lining grows in other places such as the ovaries or fallopian tubes. It isn't clear what causes the condition, but it can be truly debilitating. This was certainly the case for Hannah, who has spent her entire adulthood learning how to manage the pain and the impact on her daily life. 'I suffered from endometriosis right from my early teenage years, but I wasn't diagnosed until I was twenty-two,' she says. Hannah spent nine years in waves of crippling pain throughout her adolescence and even had her appendix removed aged fifteen, this being a frequent misdiagnosis of the condition. 'My periods were so painful that I had to take many weeks off school and university,' Hannah tells me. She even lost a job in her early twenties when the firm she was working for wouldn't support her management of the condition, not even allowing her to take in a measly hot water bottle to try and mitigate the pain.

Hannah tried various treatments for her endometriosis, including multiple hormonal therapies, exclusion diets and alternative therapies, all with minimal or fleeting success. She missed out on so much, and reflects on her twenties as a time when she should have been living her best life but simply wasn't able to do that. 'I completely lost trust in my body,' she tells me, 'and that also impacted on my mental health.' Imagine being a young person and having to sit on the sidelines, curled up in pain, watching others live the happy, carefree life which you are unable to enjoy. Hannah felt betrayed by her body and lost all confidence in being able to have the life she had dreamt of.

When Hannah began studying for her medical degree aged twenty-seven, the stress of intense study plus the unforgiving junior doctor's lifestyle meant that her symptoms got progressively worse. I can't imagine living with daily pain combined with – as Hannah describes – 'recurring intrusive thoughts' while enduring fourteen-hour nightshifts in the process of studying to become a doctor. Hannah was trapped in an endless cycle of pain and other debilitating symptoms which meant that she never felt able to live the active, healthy lifestyle that she so desperately wanted. But I guess when you collapse halfway around a 5k run because your body can't handle that on top of the chronic condition it is trying to deal with, it doesn't exactly fill you with confidence to go and kick ass with any of the en vogue fitness regimes. This is where Hannah found herself: trapped in a body which was struggling to do the bare minimum and a mind which desperately wanted to do so much more.

After two decades of struggle, Hannah ended up having a hysterectomy at the age of thirty-five – a very last resort in the management of her condition. It is known as a 'surgical menopause' and Hannah describes the impact of this and the partial removal of her endocrine (hormonal) system. 'Even though I'm a doctor, I naively thought that once I recovered from surgery, all would be well,' she says.

While recovering from her life-changing operation, she was faced with the brutal reality that her struggle wasn't over. Immediately after surgery, a physiotherapist came to see Hannah in her hospital bed with a stark warning: 'You do realise that your pelvic floor will be incredibly weak and you won't be able to run again, don't you?' Hannah was devastated at hearing this pronouncement right at the time when she was finally allowing herself to believe in building a strong body which could live a healthy and active life. This was a truly crushing blow. 'One of the reasons I'd opted to have the surgical menopause in the first place was because I wanted to have a better quality of life,' Hannah says. The fact that a person with certain medical qualifications came and dispelled that possibility for her within a matter of *hours* is quite unbelievable – and completely devastating. Hannah was in floods of tears in the hospital, not knowing whether she would finally be forced to let go of the dream she'd been holding on to for so long. 'I knew I would never be any kind of "super athlete", but I just wanted to be able to run,' she says.

I find it shocking that somebody could trample all over a person's dreams like this – especially hours after a major operation. I wonder if that person had any idea about his words and their impact? Of course, it might simply be the case that his words were particularly clumsy and ill-considered, and he didn't actually mean that – literally – Hannah would never be able to run again. But words matter, don't they? The words he chose on that day were so final and conclusive, definitively confirming that Hannah 'couldn't' run again. Not that she might find the journey to start running after her operation 'challenging' or 'difficult', or that it might prove to be a 'lengthy and arduous' journey. Instead, just those two dreadful words: 'YOU CAN'T'. Having lived with such a crippling, chronic illness for so long and finally seeing a chink of light, it seems mindless that a vulnerable person would then see somebody streamroller over their dreams – as modest as they were. 'It makes you realise as a health care professional that you need to be really careful with both *what* and *how* you communicate,' Hannah says.

Regardless, this is where Hannah found herself. Recovering from a surgical menopause, aged thirty-five, having just been told that she will never run again. And let's remember the other major impact of Hannah's surgery: she would never be able to have children. Absolutely not. Unequivocally. Knowing that there would be no reversal and zero possibility of becoming a mother in the future (obvious adoption or surrogacy caveats apply), the true impact of this is huge. 'I made the decision to have the operation because my quality of life was so poor,' she says.

Having never been able to fully commit to a long-term training or exercise programme before due to her permanently relapsing symptoms, Hannah made her choice to undergo a surgical menopause based on the life she wanted to live. 'I felt so poorly – both physically and mentally – before the surgery that I never even considered that I would be physically capable of having children,' she says. 'I genuinely couldn't see how I could look after a child, so it felt like I had no option.' Hannah goes on to talk about how dealing with this reality hasn't been linear, and although many times she has felt absolutely fine about the prospect of not having any children, she has suffered more with the impact of this as she has grown older. Some days she is fine; other days it weighs heavily on her heart. As with any complex emotional situation, the path can be rocky with unexpected twists and turns. It simply isn't true to say that Hannah has been able to deal absolutely with the prospect of never having children. More honestly, she has struggled at times in the years since her operation, oscillating between conflicting emotions.

I was fortunate enough to have my daughter, and I can't begin to imagine the whirlpool of emotions that come with a battle like Hannah's, ultimately having that choice taken away. In a world which so often likes to box people in and label them, Hannah disappointingly found this to be true. 'I was once on a child-free podcast and the people interviewing me were shocked when I admitted that sometimes not being able to have children still makes me sad,' she says. What – she should be glad about the fact?! If only people were more accepting about the complexities around circumstances like Hannah's, rather than feeling the need to judge and to stigmatise.

Following the surgery, it took Hannah longer to recuperate than she had expected. 'I recovered relatively quickly from a physical point of view, but it took far longer from a mental health perspective,' she says. She didn't work for several months after the surgery, as she struggled to find a hormone replacement therapy which her body could absorb. Being a female without any oestrogen isn't much fun, and Hannah battled with a range of symptoms including aching joints and increased anxiety while her medication was adjusted.

Eventually, as she began to heal, Hannah started to increase her activity levels, and the following summer she completed the Couch to 5k training plan. 'I remember feeling absolutely elated when I completed the 5k,' she says. 'I wasn't in any pain [which she had been while running prior to the operation] and I felt … ' – she takes a moment to consider her choice of words – 'hopeful.'

The enormity of that word isn't lost on me. It is the very thing that was almost taken from Hannah – for so long she was without any hope of her body being able to function without pain, and then following her operation she almost gave up hope once again when a medical professional stamped on her dreams with clumsy words. This was a big deal. And while following that Couch to 5k training plan, another amazing thing happened. Hannah had always struggled with debilitating fatigue, explaining that this was like an omnipresent fog which shrouded her life. 'I discovered that as long as I wasn't overdoing things, I actually found that I had more energy – and running wasn't depleting me.' This came after decades of real fear about exacerbating her symptoms and making her feel even worse. This must have been a real Eureka moment for Hannah: to realise that running moderately *gave her energy*, which sounds counter-intuitive, but which we know to be true.

Hannah's very own running revolution had begun.

She began turning up to her local Parkrun, and before long she decided to train for the Brighton Marathon in 2017. All the while, she continued to make the connection between her improving energy levels and those things which aided her in managing her condition – primarily running and a focus on healthy nutrition. Hannah's marathon journey was littered with challenges, including a sprained ankle and a stress fracture, and so sadly she was unable to make it to the start line of the marathon. But that didn't matter. Although Hannah was truly gutted that she couldn't run the marathon, she was already feeling the benefits of the many months of sustained training and the positive ways her body was responding (other than the injuries, of course!). She noticed that when she didn't run, she found handling stress much more difficult, and she began to trust in her body after many years of doubt. The belief that started to grow following the months of increased mileage allowed Hannah to change the story she had once believed about her own body and its capabilities.

How many of us can relate to this? Throughout writing this book I have spoken to so many people who have told me, 'I wasn't a very sporty kid at school' or 'I never thought of myself as "a runner"'. I know that feeling very well. Isn't it funny how easy it is for us to believe that story about ourselves and how difficult it is to change it? But – as I have discovered since sharing my own story – it happens all the time to those of us who were never runners, those of us who were always 'at the back of the pack'. It is so possible to rewrite that script – just as Hannah was beginning to discover. And when the realisation finally hits, it can be life-changing. To think that you are no longer confined to the sidelines, watching other people live the active life which you felt unable to be a part of; to feel like you now have access to that lifestyle and to those things that you used to watch other people do: running marathons being one such thing. You can be a part of that now! It's yours for the taking. It is like finding a Wonka golden ticket – only this time, the tickets aren't restricted to just five particularly fortunate individuals; they are available to anyone. You just have to go out and grab one.

Hannah and I briefly discuss the well-intentioned fear of those closest to us who consider that we are pushing ourselves too hard. Hannah mentions her mum – her 'greatest champion' – who on occasion has suggested that she is taking on a little too much. I've experienced the same thing with my dad, who has always believed that running a marathon is 'silly' and it is simply too far for me to run. It's difficult, because those views can permeate. We can internalise them and start to question the newfound belief which made our lofty goals seem possible. And even more difficult is the fact that these opinions are from the people who love us. They don't want to see us break ourselves – or worse. It is certainly a difficult balance to strike: taking on board the concerns of others while not allowing their fear to destroy our dreams before we have even begun.

To help with this, Hannah has surrounded herself with people who inspire her and who have helped to change the narrative around what it is possible to achieve. She tells me about a good friend who has suffered two bouts of breast cancer and yet has defied the odds and completed a half-Ironman distance (1.2-mile swim, 56-mile bike ride and 13.1-mile run). These people exist! They live down our road and they run past us on the street. In fact, since opening my eyes to the many incredible stories of running and resilience, I've come to realise that these people are *everywhere*! Listen to the stories of people in your local running club. Hang out at the nearest Parkrun. I guarantee that most of the people there will have their own stories about superhuman effort and overcoming adversity. All you need to do is to talk to people and listen. For Hannah, listening to her friend's story has inspired her to keep going when doubt might otherwise have crept in through the back door.

It may be that both Hannah and I are dealing with an older generation who were brought up to believe that women weren't capable of running these kinds of distances; that it was too physically demanding even for professional athletes, let alone 'everyday' runners like the pair of us. Remember that it wasn't until 1984 that women were finally able to run the marathon distance at the Olympics. That is within both my and Hannah's lifetime. Our parents grew up with the unfounded presumption that long-distance running was dangerous to our health. Of course, not everyone from that generation is of the same mindset, but I know that both Hannah and I have experienced the protective, misguided fear of one or both parents who see marathon running as taking an unnecessary risk. We need the likes of Hannah's friend and, indeed, Hannah herself to dispel this myth and to rewrite the story around long-distance running for women like us. However, Hannah says that it is equally important to remind women that they're not a failure if they *don't* run marathons. This is a really important point, because not everybody has to run a marathon or complete an Ironman. It doesn't make their efforts or achievements any less valid. So, as Hannah rightly points out, it is a difficult balance to strike.

Following her stress fracture, Hannah was able to remind herself that she had already overcome far worse obstacles, which helped her to mentally reframe her recovery into just another challenge rather than seeing it as a huge setback. She did the sensible thing and started to work on her strength and mobility before starting to run again. This is great advice for anyone who has suffered an injury, and Hannah worked hard to regain the strength in her ankles before asking her body to handle the high impact of running. In fact, focusing on strength work enabled Hannah to come back stronger, and she went on to complete the Cambridge Half Marathon in 2020. 'I did better than I expected,' she says. After entering the race at least four times previously but being unable to take up her place (one year because she couldn't change a hospital shift!), Hannah actually made it to the start line. 'I arrived on race day ready and raring to go!' she says. 'I ran with my friend Anna, and it was a fantastic day. I loved running around the old colleges and cobbled streets, and the crowd's cheers helped spur us on. Having thought I wouldn't even get the chance to start the race, I was delighted to finish in just under two hours.' Another mini win for Hannah in her battle with the 'you can't do this' demons.

Hannah tells me about one of her memorable runs earlier in the summer. 'I went out for my long Sunday run. Although I always enjoy these runs, it's fair to say that they often feel like a bit of an effort after the one-hour mark. However, on this day, I forgot about my watch and simply immersed myself in my surroundings. It was a beautiful morning, and the sun was bright. I noticed – *really* noticed – the things that I'd passed on the same route previously: the deep green colour of the leaves as I ran through a wood and a host of multicoloured poppies amongst some shale and rubble. I remember feeling incredibly peaceful and as though I could run for hours.'

Hannah has learnt to make the very best of what she's got and she has rewritten the story she once told herself about her own capabilities.

Since sharing her story with me, Hannah tells me that she would still love to run a marathon one day. 'So far, my marathon plans have been thwarted by injury,' she says. 'It's frustrating, but also makes me all the more determined.' Ultimately though, Hannah's overriding goal is to be able to run regularly and for many years to come. 'My husband and I are relocating to Norwich, and I am looking forward to joining a local running group there and meeting new people. I would love to get into trail running, and to run along the Norfolk coast. Being in nature nourishes my soul.'

# FELICITY

Like so many of the people whose stories I have listened to in the process of writing this book, Felicity's introduction to me is rather an apologetic one. I'm getting used to the 'Hi Rachel, I hope I'm not wasting your time, because my story isn't all that exciting' preamble to an interview, and in most instances, I've discovered that these are where the most impactful stories are to be found. A pattern seems to be emerging where those people who perceive that there is 'nothing special' about their stories are the ones that resonate with me the most. Is this also true of life more generally? I would hazard a guess that it is. 'Those who shout the loudest ... ' and all that.

So, here we are again. I press record on our Zoom call, and I've already heard the familiar caveat that this will be *the* dullest 'so what?' story vaguely related to running and mental wellbeing *ever*. I hate to tell Felicity this so early in our call, but I know that she is wrong. What's more, this is the very essence of the book that I am now writing! This is the reason why I felt so compelled to hunt down those stories of everyday strength and resilience which we never hear about. I became so jaded with scrolling through the latest Instagram highlights showing me absolutely nothing of interest that I decided to go and look for these stories myself. Felicity is one of the people I was fortunate enough to find. Her posts would – I guess – never hit the kind of audience to warrant featuring on *today's Insta recommends/ trending for you* lists. Depressingly, mine for today consists of an airbrushed selfie of Amanda Holden and a tiny dachshund with adorable big brown eyes dressed in a woolly hat. At least the image of the sausage dog makes me smile. Don't get me started on the other ...

Anyway, I'm familiar with this pattern. I've heard it all before.

Felicity tells me that she began running in March 2017. She seems very keen to focus on the running, but I get the feeling there is a lot more to her story. I begin by asking her why she started running at this time. Her answer? 'Because my wife left me in autumn 2016.' Rather like the Brexit referendum (which happened in the same year), she tells me, 'It was somewhat unexpected.'

Told you. Felicity's story is already fascinating, and I can't wait to find out more.

Felicity is a young, attractive, intelligent, successful gay woman living in a small rural community in northern England. We'll come on to talk about that later, but for now, we need to know more about Felicity and her journey. 'I was only thirty-one at the time [my marriage] ended and I felt like such a failure,' she says.

It would be easy to skim over the months from autumn 2016 to the time when Felicity's running journey first began, but I don't want to do that. I can sense that she is far happier talking to me about her running journey than she is trawling through her painful memories of a marriage ending which caused her life – and her confidence – to come crashing down around her ankles. But that isn't a true account of her story. It isn't a fair reflection of *anyone's* story who has been through an emotionally devastating relationship break-up. A heartbroken person doesn't get to just wish away a few months of their life and potter around the house while waiting for the aching sadness to disappear. It doesn't work like that (although it would be much easier if it did).

Felicity is galloping ahead, but I need to bring her back. This is a pain that many of us know, and I don't want it to be swept under the carpet without any acknowledgement or explanation. In between telling me about her different race goals, Felicity talks about her mental state at the time.

'I was living on my own for the first time in my life,' she says. And then it happens: I can see what the end of Felicity's marriage did to her. She felt utterly and completely alone. I know that she would far rather I write about her first 10k, which led to a half-marathon, which went on to … and so forth – and I will come on to that. But first, this needs unpicking.

Loneliness. Being alone. Returning from a long day at work to a cold, empty house with no lights on and no cars in the drive. Nothing is cooking on the hob, just a few cold leftovers sit on a shelf in the fridge. You wonder what you'll do on yet another yawning weekend which will drag on until you have another conversation with a human being next to the coffee machine at work on Monday. Yes, I've read *Eleanor Oliphant* (it's a great book) and her fictitious character is very different to Felicity, but they have one thing in common. Both know all about loneliness. They know it so fucking well. Intimately, in fact. And Felicity became very familiar with loneliness in autumn 2016 when her wife left her.

I once worked for a charity which was based in a deprived part of the town where I lived, and my job was to run a project based around tackling loneliness and social isolation in the community which was (rightly) being treated as an emerging health crisis. Without writing a thesis on the subject – which I could – it is worth pointing out a few important facts. Firstly, when we talk about loneliness and social isolation, we are talking about two closely related but separate factors. Loneliness is *subjective*. A person can *feel* lonely anywhere: they can be in a room full of people and feel lonely; they can live on their own and be perfectly happy. Social isolation, on the other hand, is *objective*: a person may not have contact with very many people during their everyday life and this can lead to fewer opportunities for interaction. It's a subtle yet important difference. In this regard, both loneliness and social isolation contribute to many serious physical and mental health ailments, including:

- an increased risk of cardiovascular disease (Barth et al., 2010)[3]
- reduced cognitive functioning (Shankar et al., 2013)[4]
- immune dysregulation (Jaremka et al., 2013)[5]
- an increased risk of hypertension (Hawkley et al., 2010)[6]
- an increased risk of depression (Cacioppo et al., 2006).[7]

In addition, there is convincing evidence that loneliness and social isolation are significant risk factors for mortality, comparable to other well-established risk factors such as smoking (Holt-Lunstad et al., 2015).[8]

So, I'm keen to explore this part of Felicity's story – when she is trying to push past the icky, uncomfortable bit and on to the 'fun part' when she is past the pain, she has discovered running and her loneliness is no more. But I want to know how she got there. I want to know how she shifted from both loneliness and social isolation to the life she is living today. I think this is important for several reasons.

Firstly, let's look at the loneliness aspect of Felicity's experience. She found herself living alone for the first time ever. This is *huge*. Never before had she been the only person to put the bins out, to draw the curtains and pay the bills. She had lived with her parents (obviously) and then friends while at university. Following that, she had met her ex-wife and they set up a home together. Aged thirty-one, Felicity found herself listening to the sound of absolute silence for the first time in her life. That is a terrifying prospect for anybody. We are social creatures, and we depend on others for so much of our mental and physical wellbeing. It is no secret that elderly people who are isolated go to visit their GP at times not for any ailment in particular, but because deep down they want – they *need* – human contact. This is a well-known aspect of human behaviour. *We need people!* And when a key person in your life is suddenly taken away – or when they have taken themselves away – the result can be catastrophic. Felicity says, 'I had many evenings thinking, "How do I fill my time?"'

And as I write this chapter, it is mid-August. This is a particularly difficult time for Felicity, as she explains that this is the same month that her wife left her. 'It's a funny time, isn't it?' she muses. 'Most people are going away or on holiday with the kids, but because I don't have children, August is a weird, low time for me.' Think about that for a second. Pre-Covid, there's every chance that many of us would be busy planning our survival for the six-week school holidays while counting down the days until we could escape for some Mediterranean sunshine and cocktails on the beach. Felicity's wife left her at the beginning of August when the rest of the world was about to go away on the family holiday – whether at home or abroad. How would that feel? 'I can remember wishing that it was winter so that I could sit on the train and no one would see me cry,' she says, admitting that the recollection of that memory makes her feel sad. 'I can remember walking home from the train station and keeping my shit together, then as soon as I opened my front door I sat on the stairs and sobbed for hours.' Felicity managed to hold it together when she had to – in front of work colleagues and rail passengers – but when she got home, the sadness overwhelmed her.

It makes perfect sense. It was August – the beginning of the summer holidays. Felicity's wife had just left her, and she was desperately lonely.

Furthermore, looking at Felicity's situation objectively, it is perfectly legitimate to reason that she might be socially isolated. She is a gay woman living in a rural village. I'm not being funny, but it's hardly Soho, is it? How many attractive, eligible, single, like-minded gay females do you reckon might be living in a tiny, northern, rural village community? As Felicity herself acknowledges, 'There aren't very many.'

Following the initial shock of her heartbreak, Felicity began to immerse herself in learning about recovery. She read books on coping strategies for painful divorces, and in doing so, she picked up a few handy hints about how to begin rebuilding her life. One of the suggested ideas was to 'do things your ex doesn't know about you'. She is quick to explain that this wasn't meant in a reactionary, 'I'll bloody show you!' pointless demonstration to the ex concerned, but simply as a way of learning to live in a completely different way.

Imagine being fearful of returning home after a day at work, knowing that the silent evening hours are likely to stretch and linger endlessly until bedtime, when the chances are that you won't sleep very well anyway. Felicity is very honest about her mindset following her divorce. Being a very career-driven person, she gave herself two options. 'I knew that I could either throw myself completely into work or I could try to work out who I was and just learn how to live.' She made a deal with herself not to regret her decision, but to make a firm one and stick with it.

She believes that she made the right choice.

Felicity explains that she didn't really 'run'. She occasionally went out for a slow twenty-minute jog around the block, but she wasn't – in her mind – a 'runner'. Running is not something she would ever have aligned herself with in her previous life. She decided to take a little pressure off her working life and to go running a few evenings during the week as a way of filling time – to do something with the empty, yawning hours until nightfall. 'It helped me to put some structure into my non-working hours,' Felicity says, and she goes on to describe this as being a 'transferable skill' in that, by doing so with running, she was able to find ways to shape the rest of her free time.

I take a moment to think about Felicity's motivations to begin running and create a new life for herself following her painful divorce, and it strikes me that parts of my own story resonate with hers. On the face of it, we have little in common, but once you dig a bit deeper, it's all there: the need to redefine ourselves and to seek out those parts of us which we have never yet seen. Perhaps it's both of us asking, 'Who can we be?' as opposed to, 'Who are we right now?' Running enabled us to do that.

Felicity says, 'Running became a bridge from my old life to my new life.' I think this is such powerful imagery. Bridges are generally considered to be strong; they take you across otherwise inhospitable terrain – we wouldn't get very far wading across the Thames! A bridge takes you to a destination. You start out at point A and the bridge can guarantee your arrival at point B – even if you don't know where that is yet. There might be shark-infested waters underneath, but you can trust in the bridge to get you there safely. So, okay, enough of the bridge analogies. My point is that Felicity trusted in running to take her to a place she didn't know – to a life that didn't yet exist. She trusted that running would somehow take her away from the sadness and the loneliness of the cold, dark evenings and on to a brighter place. She trusted in the journey that running would take her on. Isn't that incredible?

Setting herself a new running schedule during the week and again at weekends gave Felicity a feeling of control back in her life. Following circumstances that were entirely outside her control, choosing to create a routine and stick with it was Felicity's way of counteracting the feelings of helplessness which could have engulfed her following the ending of her marriage. This is empowering; it demanded that she make a personal commitment to change and to do all the other things necessary to adhere to her new schedule. Answering simple, logistical questions such as 'When will I need to eat? Before or after I run?' made it possible for Felicity to redesign her life to fit the goal that she had set for herself. Running had a knock-on effect in other areas of her life, too: she no longer dreaded the endless summer weekends when days stretched ever longer and she had no idea how to fill the hours. Enter stage left: the long run. Felicity was now back in control of her own life. She was giving herself the responsibility to create her future and the accountability to stick with it.

Felicity isn't a member of a running club, but she does have some close friends who she runs with. Once she began running, she initially questioned her previous assumptions that she was an extrovert who hated being on her own. 'I realised that I actually enjoy running by myself,' she says, as though this was the first time she had even considered that she could enjoy her own company. What a revelation! For a person who had once feared solitude, running allowed Felicity to embrace it fully and to not pine for the company of another person to make her feel whole. I absolutely love this. We're not all the same; some of us do need the support of a club and to run alongside others, but for many of us, solo runs are meditative and restorative. 'I just listen to music and then I lose myself in running,' Felicity tells me. She returns home from a run and wonders where the last two hours have gone. If that isn't meditation, then I don't know what is. 'That's good for me because it means that my mind can stop whirring.'

I've run alone for many years and I've also enjoyed many years of running with a club and with people I met there, some of whom became very close running companions. I wouldn't wish any of it had been different, and I'm realising that I need both the solitude of running and the companionship of others. There is a place for both. Felicity might involve herself more in the running community in the future, but for now, she is very aware of her own needs.

We talk about the virtual running community and I ask Felicity her thoughts on that. She took part in the 2020 virtual London Marathon – her first marathon – and she describes how she found inspiration through the online running community and from learning about inspiring women such as Kathrine Switzer – the first woman to officially run the Boston Marathon in 1967, who was famously manhandled off the course by the race organiser (although she managed to complete the race nonetheless). 'I found reading about other female marathon runners very inspirational,' she says.

Felicity's very first marathon should have been a very different experience. Pre-Covid, she would have stood alongside another 50,000 people (myself one of them) on the appropriate start line at Blackheath. She would have been completely immersed in the magnitude of the event, with the multicoloured swarms of runners, the excitement of running chatter and the hot air balloons swaying over the heath. She would have no doubt had a similar experience to the one I had back in 2011 when I experienced the true joy of running the London Marathon for the very first time. Instead, Felicity was faced with the prospect of running her own virtual marathon – just like the rest of us.

'I remember being very grumpy about it for a while,' she says, but then she managed to reframe the situation to help her get through the many challenges of lockdown. 'We were in Tier 1 when I ran the virtual London Marathon,' she tells me, 'and my friends helped me a lot.' She stands up and reaches across her desk to pick up an enormous white sheet which opens out to reveal 'FELICITY'S MARATHON!' written in brightly coloured paint. Felicity's friends made the banner and helped her to organise a local route, together with scheduling various changeover points and support along the way. They made sure that she was never on her own – they were permitted to run together up to a maximum of three at any one time, so the checkpoints offered the chance for one person to switch and for somebody else to be her support crew for a few more miles. Felicity's friends also organised non-running support along the route, which Felicity refers to as her 'cheer points'. 'It was a bit hectic on the day,' she says, 'and I felt sorry for my running friend who ran the last thirteen miles with me, because I didn't feel much like talking by that point!'

Felicity completed her virtual marathon and she was never alone. Sadly, one of her closest friends was unable to join her for any of the miles due to being in self-isolation, but Felicity tells me that the route went past her house several times, and on each lap she got a huge boost of energy from seeing her friend through the window jumping up and down frantically in support. What's more, Felicity's parents were unable to watch her run the marathon because of the pandemic, and so they had to make do with a WhatsApp video of her running across a virtual finishing line. If this isn't an example of a classic '2020 Covid Marathon' then I don't know what is. On that day, I was running my own virtual London Marathon from my front door, with my husband and daughter moving to various points on the route for support. My favourite part was running past our house at miles nine and twenty-two with a pasting table set up outside and a buffet of energy-boosting goodies, plus Tilly's tiny toy mice who came out to join the support crew. I wonder how many other thousands of variations there are on this theme. It's incredible to think of the many ingenious ways people decided to run their own London Marathon – most of which were nowhere near the city of London. But we *still* got out there and we still ran 26.2 miles, didn't we? That's how much running the marathon meant to people like me and Felicity. We brought family and friends in to help us plan and to support us – even those who were isolating like Felicity's friend. I find it inspiring to think that even when the event itself could no longer take place, collectively we love running too much to let Covid – or anything else for that matter – put an end to our marathon dreams. 'It was certainly memorable!' Felicity says. I second that!

So, running offered Felicity a way to rebuild her life by filling a void which had been left by the ending of her marriage. That's one aspect of her recovery. But what about her self-confidence? How did running help to rebuild Felicity's belief in herself and enable her to face the prospect of returning to the dating scene and filling in the *non-running* aspects of her life? 'Running was a huge factor in reinventing myself after the break-up,' she says. 'It made me feel good about myself again physically.' She refers to a holiday snap which she posted on Facebook of her wearing a bikini, which she would *never* have done before. 'Yeah, I know I look good!' was her comedy caption for the post. Hell, why not? Why shouldn't she be proud of the stronger, leaner, firmer body that she now had thanks to running? 'And when I was fearful of doing something, I thought to myself, "Well, if you can run 26.2 miles, then you can do this – whatever it might be."'

Running helped Felicity to reframe other obstacles which at one time might have held her back. Confidence is so multifaceted and means different things to different people, but for Felicity, she gained confidence in her own body and was able to see past her fears and turn obstacles into mini hurdles to get over rather than allow them to fester into a negative mindset without the possibility of finding a way forward. We both agree that the feeling of running a marathon has opened the floodgates for possibility to enter our lives in ways we hadn't considered before.

What about friendships? How was Felicity able to fill the gap left by her Person? You know – the one who fills all your needs, and when they leave you there is a hole the size of a meteorite left in your life. 'When my wife left me, I didn't really know anyone in my home town,' she says. 'We had done the whole "moving to a new town as a couple" thing.' Felicity recalls thinking about her situation and how challenging it might be to unpick the damage and to find other people to befriend within her community. She describes a moment of terror at that prospect and having to rationally tell herself to calm down. I've been there. I know how it feels to lose yourself completely within a relationship to the extent that you're known only as a duo and the world shrinks to fit. You don't always realise it's happening at the time, and regardless of the longevity of that partnership, I've learnt from experience that it's far healthier to have a balanced life containing other friendships.

Gradually, as Felicity began running and incorporating other activities into her life, she started to make new friends and to build her social support network up from ground zero. 'I can't even imagine not having my group of friends now,' she says, her eyes widening in a look of disbelief at the insular life she led before.

And let's look at the facts. Not only did Felicity have to build a friendship group from scratch, but she doesn't live near any members of her close family. When the break-up happened, life was – dare I even say the word – 'normal'. But then we have just experienced eighteen months of lockdown where people just like Felicity have been even more socially isolated than they were before. This could have been catastrophic for Felicity's mental health had she chosen 'option 1' and simply decided to focus on pursuing her already successful career (and, by the way, she is *still* working from home eighteen months later). Thank goodness she chose the second option. Thank goodness she was brave and took the baby steps towards rebuilding her life in a more balanced way, and to allow other people to come into it, people who could and would support her – not only while she ran the virtual London Marathon in her hometown, but every day since.

The truth is, we need to share parts of ourselves with other people across a variety of social settings. We need to look up and outwards when it might feel easier to look inwards at ourselves in our ever-decreasing comfortable bubble. Felicity has certainly learnt that lesson. 'I'll never make that mistake again,' she says. To think that running has been the catalyst for Felicity to make changes to this aspect of her life is nothing short of miraculous. For running to have enabled her to piece her life back together, and more than that, to help it *grow* again, is phenomenal.

One of the many things I admire about Felicity is her bravery and her honesty in talking about her experience. While sharing her journey on social media, she is keen to point out that her ability to completely turn her life around comes with effort. 'I try,' she says. Those two words are so powerful. 'I try every single day.' She has received messages from those who find her story inspirational, and while she is flattered by such commentary, Felicity would rather people know how many deliberate choices she makes every single day to keep moving forwards. 'Take this morning,' she says. 'I made myself get out of bed. Of course, I would rather have just stayed there. It's the same with running and with eating healthily. Every single choice I make is a deliberate, very conscious one.'

I think this is an important point to acknowledge. This stuff hasn't suddenly become easy for Felicity. A magic switch hasn't just flicked, making all the positive steps so much more manageable. She still has to try! I want to acknowledge that, because Felicity has got to where she is now with a huge amount of effort. Not once or a few times, but every single day. Guess what the analogy is here? It's running again, isn't it? To become a better runner, to train for a marathon, you need to consistently take steps forward every day – even resting on rest days (which can feel like an effort, right?!). What comes first? Having the consistency to build a healthy, sustainable life, or consistency in running? For Felicity, I think we can safely say that the running came first. Having a training routine and sticking with it day in, day out, regardless of any possible reason or excuse not to, has paved the way for Felicity to use those same principles in the rest of her life. Discipline and consistency works. Sitting at home wishing things were different doesn't. And it works in every aspect of life. *I WILL hang up these clothes which otherwise might stay in a pile on the floor … I WILL vacuum the lounge because I want to live in a clean space … I WILL have a shower and put on some make-up this morning because I value myself enough to do that and I want to reflect that confidence in my appearance, today.* These are all tiny sparks of progress which were borne from Felicity's decision to start running. I don't think it's any exaggeration to state that by changing her mindset in this way, she was able to transform her life.

We talk about the way that constantly and deliberately moving forward has enabled both of us to build confidence in ourselves and fulfil our own commitments. *I CAN keep that promise I made to myself. I CAN commit to something and stick with it. I CAN see this marathon training plan through to its conclusion.* We slowly begin to believe in our own resolve and we no longer accept the lame excuses for reneging on a goal we had set for ourselves – even one as simple as getting out of the front door and going for a run. This is *huge*! It redefines the boundaries of what we will accept from ourselves. Perhaps our previous response on a drizzly Sunday morning of rolling over and opting for a bacon sarnie is no longer acceptable. *I WILL put on my running shoes and I WILL go out for a run.* That is the deal I have made with myself and so that is what I will do. This is exactly the mindset that I adopted when I set myself the challenge to run the London Marathon following the birth of my daughter. Throughout those seven months I had thousands of opportunities to break my own contract – the deal I had made with myself. I could have decided for a million different reasons not to go along to the next stage of my plan, but all the while, my inner strength and resolve was growing sufficiently to enable me to fully commit. I can remember so many times when other people even tried to pull me away from my plan. 'Oh, don't bother going out running today, Rach. It's throwing it down out there!' I think this strengthened my resolve even more, perhaps because I knew that they wouldn't have made the same choice to commit to the goal on that day.

Felicity and I discuss this aspect of our journey and we agree that this allows us to trust ourselves to commit.

Felicity opens up about her sexuality and the impact that running has had on her personal life. 'I was twenty-eight when I got married and it all felt very traditional,' she says, explaining that at that time, gay couples had to make do with a civil partnership as marriage hadn't been legalised. 'It was very conventional and we planned to have children.' When Felicity's marriage ended, she had to consider the prospect that the traditional 'happy family' she thought she had signed up for was perhaps not going to happen. 'I am thirty-six and I've had to come to terms with the fact that my life may not look like I thought it would.' Felicity goes on to talk about how running has helped her to process her new reality. 'Running has shown me that things may have turned out pretty differently to how I envisaged my life would be, but that's okay.'

Wow! I replay Felicity saying this during our interview and I can feel the hairs on the back of my neck stand on end. Running has enabled Felicity to accept the way her life is different to how she once expected, and it has allowed her to consider things in a more adaptable way. Running is helping her to flow with life instead of sticking to some rigid notion of how she believed her life should look.

I ask Felicity how she thinks her life might be different had she never started out on her running journey. Initially, she seems taken aback. 'That's such a big question!' she says. I agree. I ask it not to force her to stare down a bleak rabbit hole of hopelessness and muse on all the horror that might have ensued. I ask Felicity that question because, genuinely, there would have been an alternative life to the one Felicity chose.

'Initially, I considered moving down to London,' she tells me, explaining that's what other people seem to do in a crisis. 'Or I thought about moving back to the place where I used to live, or even to another city, because rural locations aren't exactly awash with single, gay women.' Instead of leaving, Felicity decided to stay in the house she bought with her ex, right on the edge of the beautiful Peak District where she loves to go running. And she's so glad she did. 'Running has given me the confidence to be on my own and to make new friends. I genuinely don't know what my alternative life might have looked like.'

After a few more moments, Felicity considers that she might have indeed thrown herself into work – as in reverted to option 1 – and furthered her career, which was going well at the time (and still is). Interestingly, Felicity tells me that there was a work opportunity which she was expected to take, but she declined in favour of option 2. 'I seriously don't regret making that decision,' she says, explaining that her life is so much fuller now in every possible way and she no longer has the prospect of a yawning weekend looming ahead without any plans other than waiting for Monday morning to arrive. Felicity could so easily have thrown herself into her career and spent her Friday evenings with her head stuck in spreadsheets. She might have worked on a project on Sundays rather than prepare herself for a long training run. But what a sad and lonely existence that might have been. Instead, she has forced her way through the darkness and emerged into the brightest sunshine with her new group of friends, her running goals and the life she has created, which is filled with joy and purpose. I think Felicity is an inspiration to anyone who has found themselves either feeling or being alone, in whatever circumstance – showing them that by simply putting on a pair of trainers, they too can find the light.

Since sharing her story with me, Felicity has completed the 2021 London Marathon. 'It was the hardest run I have ever done, for reasons I still don't understand; it just wasn't my day, but it was still the London Marathon! Somehow, I made it round, and I actually beat my previous year's virtual marathon time by twenty minutes and raised a lot of money for Diabetes UK in the process,' she says. Felicity tells me that she is taking some time out to allow her legs to recover, and in the medium term to let her mind recover. 'I have actually just made a (positive and proactive) appointment with a therapist, to check in with myself, and make sure I know where I want to head in life.' It's great that Felicity is prioritising taking care of her mental health in this way.

# JUDI

Judi's face appears on my screen and makes me smile almost instantly. As with all these interviews, I'm never quite sure what to expect. It's always lovely to meet the person whose story I am about to hear, to see their face and to hear their voice for the first time. I soon realise that Judi doesn't pull any punches. She is a force of nature and launches straight into her story. There is no breaking the ice with any unnecessary small talk.

'Okay, so what happened to me is that on 14 September 2008 my husband, David, went out on his bike and he died on the way to church.'

I don't think I will ever get used to hearing people telling me such things. I doubt whether I will ever truly know what to say or how best to respond. What I have learnt is that I am simply here to listen, and it's only natural that I would be shocked hearing a story like this. Then she tells me his age. 'David was forty-six when he died.'

Silence. Just that. Complete silence.

I am forty-three years old. My husband is in his early fifties. Judi's husband was just a few years older than I am now when he set off on his bike one perfectly ordinary Sunday morning, and he never came home again. I really, honestly, am lost for words. *How does this happen?* How does a person who is seemingly fit and well – at least to the best of their knowledge – go out of the front door one day and drop dead without any warning, without any freak accident occurring, *without any explanation*? Only one word comes to mind: shock.

At the post-mortem, it was discovered that one of the tiny arteries in David's heart had failed. There was absolutely no chance of saving him.

'At least I had no "what-ifs",' Judi says. 'He hadn't died by suicide, there was no pain or suffering, no long-term sickness, and there was nothing that could have been done to save him.'

Judi's ability to turn this fact into a saving grace is extraordinary, but she still lost her husband. I get a distinct feeling that Judi has been more able to come to terms with David dying in this way than if – for example – he had suffered a long and painful illness or had died in some horrendous accident. Instead, the finality and the *inevitability* of David's death is a small comfort to Judi, who realises that, rationally, he would have died anyway. She says, 'It could easily have been whilst he was sitting in the armchair at home or at his desk at work, but the outcome would have been the same.' There would have been no opportunity for intervention. 'Our children were aged sixteen and eighteen at the time,' Judi tells me. 'The eighteen-year-old was about to start university.'

Dear God. The shock waves just keep coming. Can you imagine being a teenager at a crucial stage in your life when you receive the news one Sunday morning that your dad has just died while out on a bike ride? And Judi was the person who was there, at home, left picking up the pieces of not one, not two, but *three* broken hearts. And this was all happening too soon. People aren't supposed to just drop down dead aged forty-six, are they? Not without any warning. When does that happen? Yes, I know that all manner of abysmal fates befall people all the time – but when you hear it so starkly, so matter-of-factly, it sounds like some horror story you're reading that you desperately want to put down because you know it will give you nightmares.

Judi has had many years to process her grief, to come to terms with the loss of her husband and to piece her own and her children's lives back together again – and I am desperate to know how and where she began, and the role that running plays in that journey.

Before we come on to talk about Judi's recovery, she tells me a little about her mental health prior to David's death. 'I think it's fair to say that I did suffer from some mental health issues before David died,' she tells me. I find Judi's openness and her ability to reflect on her own mental health journey fascinating. She is not just reflecting on how she rebuilt herself from

September 2008, but on those issues that might have played a significant role in how she lived her life even before then. 'I think my mental health struggles were always there,' she says. 'I still receive counselling to deal with those underlying issues and how they have impacted on my life.'

I am so pleased that Judi is willing to be open about the fact that she receives counselling, not just for the grief that she has suffered, but for her underlying mental health issues, too. I find such strength in this, and I believe that people like Judi are helping to destigmatise mental health illness, however it manifests in a person's life – whether somebody has experienced a catastrophe like Judi has, or not.

We jump into the time machine, back to Judi's life before September 2008. 'I had such a wonderful life,' she tells me. 'I was working as a teaching assistant, which I loved; David had a good job, and the kids were happy. We were bobbing along nicely, working our way through to retirement, when out of nowhere, we hit the brick wall.' We know what she means by 'brick wall': David would no longer be with Judi or the children for the rest of their journey – they would have to go it alone.

Shortly before that happened, David and Judi were chatting one evening when he said to her out of the blue, 'You know, you've always got your foundation degree to fall back on if you ever need it.' He was referring to Judi's foundation teaching qualification, which she had obtained some years before. Three weeks later, David was dead. After writing the last sentence, I reflect on it, thinking that it perhaps sounds a bit stark, too shocking – but those are the exact words Judi has used.

Judi took her late husband's advice and converted her foundation degree, ultimately qualifying as a teacher, but things didn't go quite as planned. 'I couldn't get a job,' she says. 'It was terrible. I couldn't get a job anywhere, and then my dad got dementia.' Judi's confidence was at an all-time low. She found herself a widow in her mid-forties, she was unable to find employment in her chosen career after she had worked so hard to qualify, *and* her father now had dementia.

'It felt like all of it was my fault,' Judi tells me. 'It felt like it was my fault that I couldn't get a job and it was my fault that my dad was ill. I was at rock bottom.' She was under an incredible amount of pressure, grief and self-loathing. The loss of David was only the start of it. What followed were some of the toughest years imaginable.

'David would have supported me through it,' she says. 'He would have known what to say and what to do to help me, but he wasn't there.' I think this is a particularly painful aspect of Judi's story. She had relied on her lovely husband to be her rock, her support and the person she went to with any insecurities. He made it all okay again. He made her feel as though she was good enough, and when things went wrong, it wasn't her fault. Once David had died, that pillar of support had gone and Judi's self-worth came crashing to the ground. 'He was able to wipe out any negativity,' she says. 'He could eliminate any self-doubts that I had – and it was only after he died that I realised how much I depended on him doing that for me.'

We all do it, don't we? We rely on our Special Person. Our Special Person fulfils many functions. They chat to us while we're making tea (without being sexist – my SP cooks far more than I do); they cuddle us when we feel vulnerable. They reassure us when we're feeling fragile. They know how to sensitively navigate around our emotions. In fact, thinking about it, my Special Person – my husband – is *everywhere*, supporting me in everything I do – including writing this book. Not everyone is fortunate enough to have an SP. Many people don't. But when you find yours, you cannot begin to imagine waking up one morning to suddenly find that they are gone. It boggles my mind thinking about all the tiny, insignificant things, from the internet passwords to the online channels – I wouldn't have a clue how to get access to Netflix, even though we watch it most nights. I'd have no idea how to change the leads at the back of the telly (I know – how 1990s) so we can watch Amazon Prime. On a Wednesday, my SP knows which one of the bins needs putting out – it's only one option out of two, but I still wouldn't have any idea or know what time they need to be wheeled to the edge of our drive. I'm not saying that I'm completely helpless: I cut his hair, saving him a princely £50 per month, and I change the beds – he'd get lost inside a king-size duvet cover. But my point is that *nothing* would be the same if he wasn't around. Not even changing the duvet cover when he laughs as I talk him through my life-hack for the millionth time and he still doesn't care/really want to know how to do it (turn the duvet cover inside out and go for the furthest two corners, obvs).

Just as I'm thinking about all this, the next words that come out of Judi's mouth almost make me cry. 'David was the first person to believe in me,' she says.

David was Judi's *everything*.

All of that stopped so suddenly, and without any warning, without time for Judi to adjust or to begin to figure out the things that are so simple they seem ridiculous – to think about the online shopping password and the Netflix log-in. But one day – on 14 September 2008 – Judi found out what this was really like.

Judi is in the middle of a sentence when she is suddenly disturbed by the sound of a dog barking. 'I'm sorry about that,' she says. 'She's ready to go running.'

I take this as a cue to ask Judi how she began to turn her life around following the devastation of losing David. The bark feels significant, as I will soon discover.

'Well, my son started going to Parkrun,' Judi tells me with a smile creeping over her face. 'How many times have you heard people say that?' she asks me, laughing. One day, her son, Tristan, said to his mum, 'Why don't you come along? You'd enjoy it! You can bring the dog and you won't come last.' I laugh at quite possibly the best invitation to Parkrun that I've ever heard. The following weekend, Judi printed off her barcode and went along to her local Parkrun with her beloved dog, Maggie. 'And that was it!' she says. I'm sincerely hoping this isn't the end of her story, so I check on my computer and I still have fifty minutes of audio left to transcribe. *Phew!* This was the very beginning of Judi discovering her new life.

For the first time during our conversation, Judi begins to sound emotional. 'This was when I first experienced the positivity of running,' she says. 'I was greeted at the start by people I didn't even know. I was made to feel so welcome.'

Tristan had told his mum to run with the pacer towards the back who was run/walking one minute on, one minute off. 'And like a dutiful mum, I did exactly what I'd been told,' Judi says. She ran/walked her very first Parkrun with Maggie, and she loved every minute. 'It feels a bit like my son used running as a way to help me,' she says. What a lovely thought. Not only did running itself and the immediate feeling of community and togetherness wrap Judi up in a virtual hug, but it was her son's way of guiding his mum through the heavy fog of grief. It also demonstrates how far-reaching the healing power of running can be. Tristan had obviously found some solace in running, and he identified how the supportive environment of Parkrun might be a place where his mum could also benefit.

He was right.

'When I got there, people weren't questioning why I'd come to Parkrun, they were simply saying, "It's great to see you!"' This immediate sense of acceptance and belonging meant that Judi felt at home right away. She was recognised by some of the regulars as being Tristan's mum and she was cheered across the finish line by people she had never met who were hollering, 'Come on, Tristan's mum!' It was a lovely experience for Judi, who immediately felt part of a welcoming and supportive community. But one memory in particular stands out for her. 'When I was feeling tired towards the end, a man said to me, "Don't stop. Keep going." I thought about those words, and they really resonated with me. It was as though he was telling me to keep going – to keep moving forwards with my life. It was about so much more than running.' Four words of encouragement. That's all it was, but it meant such a lot to Judi. She was able to relate those words to the rest of her life and to take that sense of positivity forward far beyond Parkrun.

We've all experienced those moments, haven't we? A few words or even just an encouraging smile from another person which can – in that moment – mean the difference between keeping going and giving up. I remember being in the last mile of the Edinburgh Half Marathon in 2015 and I'd run my heart out. I was on for a time of one hour and thirty minutes, and I began to struggle. A girl with dark hair ran up beside me – I remember it so vividly – and she said quietly, 'Come on, girl. We can do this. We've got less than a mile to go.' Whatever happened within that exchange was enough for me to keep going and I crossed the line in a personal best time of one hour, thirty minutes and forty-five seconds. Had she not been there at that very moment, I might just have thrown in the towel. She helped me on that day; part of my own personal victory was down to her. I don't know who she is – we rarely know these people – but they can make all the difference. On another occasion, a girl who I knew from my running club grabbed my hand and ran with me for the last few hundred metres of a ten-mile road race. She literally picked me up and dragged me across the finish line. Moments like this will stay with me forever. I won't ever forget experiencing that sense of human spirit and the way it can lift you up when you could otherwise so easily crumble. This was Judi's first taste of the same, and the man's words have stuck with her right up to this day. Of course, he would have no idea what his simple words of encouragement meant to her, but on that day, they meant everything.

Judi went back to Parkrun the following week and she compares the feeling she had with reaching her hand back into a bag of her favourite sweets. 'I wanted some more!' she says, with a mischievous look on her face. I can just imagine her getting caught with a hand in the cookie jar, and the thought makes me smile. 'Before I knew it, I got my red T-shirt,' she says, sounding delighted at the memory of receiving the classic 'Parkrun 50' T-shirt acknowledging the commitment and participation of those – like Judi – who keep going back for more. She would have received her 'black one' – the 'Parkrun 100' T-shirt – by now. Damn blast that Covid-19 global pandemic!

Judi was a Parkrun convert, like many millions of others across the globe, but before long she began to realise that in order to improve on her Parkrun time, she needed – and she wanted – to run during the week. Parkrun was the springboard for her to incorporate running into days other than Saturday, and she has reaped the rewards ever since. 'I had a bad day on Tuesday,' she tells me. 'Everything went wrong. My sewing went wrong [Judi is an extremely talented seamstress], my counselling session was tough and I felt all out of sorts. It got to 9.30 p.m. and do you know what I did?' I think I can hazard a guess … 'I put my running shoes on and went out for a run.' I ask her if she felt better afterwards, but the enormous smile which has spread across her face is all the answer I need.

Without the stepping-stone of Parkrun, Judi might never have had the opportunity to make the mind–body connection between running and her own mental health. She might never have experienced the feeling of sheer relief of getting out of the front door – even in the dark – and running through her anxiety, her fears and frustrations; almost like chasing them off, shooing them away down the street. And it's worth pointing out that although Judi has found such freedom and joy in the discovery of running and managing her mental health, she maintained her counselling therapy throughout. Running is now a permanent part of her support package.

I'm still wondering about the dog bark. It was like Lassie was speaking to me, saying, 'Don't forget to ask about us!' This is my chance.

'When David was alive, he wouldn't let me get a dog,' Judi tells me. 'I used to say to him, "Right, if you go first, that's what I'm going to do!"' We all know what happened next.

'I started running with my dogs and from there I became involved with CaniCross,' Judi says. 'It's very different to the Parkrun community and it can get quite competitive!'

Judi describes CaniCross being like 'trail running with dogs'. Running like the clappers down a steep trail while being pulled by excitable dogs sounds brutal to me, but Judi *loves* it! I ask her if you need to run with a certain breed of dog, and I'm told that it's open to all but there is a definite trend towards huskies and border collies at the moment. 'Huskies are popular because of the Netflix series *Game of Thrones*,' Judi tells me. I adore border collies, having once owned a beautiful red collie called Maisie who I used to love running with. It makes me feel slightly wistful. Judi has two Brittany spaniels called Maggie and Poppy. She tells me, 'You just need to have a dog that will run!' I suddenly imagine interviewing a line-up of potential pets – asking various breeds of puppies if they would be prepared to run with me and be my CaniCross partner before assessing their suitability as my pet.

Judi has had her fair share of tumbles. 'I recently fell over when we were hurtling down a tricky section of trail. I hurt my ankle, but thankfully I managed to get up and carry on running and I felt *AMAZING*!' I'm still not quite convinced that it's the sport for me, but it's clear that Judi finds a huge amount of joy in running with her dogs. It has also enabled her to access another running community where the focus is on trail running for people who love dogs. So, Judi has expanded her running horizons beyond Parkrun to involve her beloved pets. Rather than simply walking her dogs, she got herself kitted out with all the necessary gear – I'm told about the importance of getting the right harness for you and your dog, and I learn that this is key to ensuring the safety of both runners and their hounds. There are many ways of getting it wrong. It sounds fascinating!

I love Judi's spirit of adventure and her willingness to try new things. I love how open she is to exploring running within different running communities, and the fact that she doesn't let fear of the unknown hold her back. She isn't even afraid of falling on rocky trails – a quality I particularly envy – and she is able to adapt herself to different types of running by widening her experiences and learning as she goes.

I understand that the strong sense of community within both Parkrun and CaniCross has played a huge part in Judi's recovery, and I can't help wondering what the impact of the Covid pandemic has been on her when all this was taken away. 'It was interesting,' she says. 'Quite a long time before Covid hit, I started running on my own with the dogs, so I already knew I could do that and so it wasn't a strange concept for me to run by myself.' And then she got injured. 'I badly twisted my ankle during lockdown and I was out for a few months,' she says. 'That was tough.' She mentions some of the things she missed the most. 'When you're out running, you don't always talk to other people, but there's always a friendly smile or a wave. A look of encouragement or a kind gesture. I really missed that.' I find the simplicity of her observations striking.

It sinks in as she is telling me this how much those tiny moments of social contact mean to a person like Judi who lives on her own. A smile. Just that. It isn't very much, is it? I'm thinking about all the times when I've passed another runner. I always try my best to pull myself out of my own head space and say 'hi' or simply smile. Granted, when you're doing your last set of speed reps it isn't always easy, but I will continue to try and do that in the future, because now I realise that to somebody like Judi that smile or 'hello' could make a difference to the rest of their day.

Judi tells me that while she was unable to run for a few months during the height of the 2020 lockdown, she felt helpless and isolated. 'I was just at home killing time,' she says. There is a real sense of this being a frustration for Judi – as though she missed the proactivity of running; the getting up and *doing something* rather than simply passing time, waiting for … well, who knows what. I get it. Running gives you a reason to get up and go; there is a clear sense of purpose and empowerment in a decision to go outside and run. We choose to do that; nobody does it for us. Without that, life can seem to be passive, as though we are waiting for the next cue instead of making our own way forward and carving our own trail. This had an impact on Judi's mental health.

'Running has become an integral part of my life,' she says. 'After my ankle injury I couldn't wait to get back out running again.' Judi says that she goes out running in all weathers. The only exception is icy conditions. I'm with her on that.

Even Judi's alter ego as an avid seamstress has woven its way into her running (apologies for the intentional pun). 'I follow someone on social media who also loves sewing and running and I realised that she lives near me.' Fast-forward a few months and Judi and her new sewing–running friend now run together every Friday. 'We run to support each other,' she says. 'I'm very lucky because I live in the middle of nowhere. I can go out running and I'm immediately faced with rolling fields. I can hear the birdsong. Running just empties my head. It wipes the slate clean.'

Judi's story is a great example of the ripple effect of running. Just one suggestion made by her son has led to an entirely new – and now a fundamental – part of her life. Running is everywhere. She runs with her various running friends; she is now a part of different running communities. She runs with and without her two lovely dogs Maggie and Poppy (who come and say hello shortly before the end of our call. I immediately begin to google 'Brittany spaniels'). She runs because it clears her head and because she loves the productivity it brings to her day. Judi doesn't claim to be the fastest runner and she doesn't have a house filled with race medals, but at the age of fifty-nine I reckon she'd give me a run for my money if I were fastened to two excitable hounds while they were galloping down trails at speed.

I also get the feeling that Judi's life has become far richer than she ever imagined it could be. Perhaps in the early years following David's death, the bleakness and the other challenges she had to overcome didn't leave much room for positivity to grow, but now it is a different story. With the help of her son, Tristan, and her two beloved dogs, Judi has been able to create a life for herself which even she finds surprising. Whatever befalls me in my future life, I would like to think that I'd have some of Judi's spirit and that I might be leaping over tree roots on gnarly woodland trails when I'm approaching my sixties.

Since sharing her story with me, Judi has told me that she is focusing on improving her pace and CaniCross technique. Her aim going forward is to complete all the nine runs which make up the Fur Nations Cup with her dogs, but she tells me that 'perhaps my greatest dream is to run up that final hill in South Shields as a competitor in the Great North Run'.

# UNFINISHED BUSINESS

**The Boston Marathon, 16 April 2018**

The weather forecast has looked ominous. I should know – I've been checking it every hour for the last three weeks, as though staring at it around the clock will change it in some way. There are predictions of freakish monsoon-like conditions together with a prevailing headwind for the one day when it matters the most … marathon day. But this isn't just any old marathon – this is my dream marathon. The Boston Marathon. The one which required me to qualify for a coveted place on the starting line. People try for years to be where I am right now, but this isn't going to plan. Blazing sunshine was forecast for Sunday – the day *before* the marathon – and we will seemingly bask in high temperatures again on Tuesday, the day *after* the marathon. But on the *ONE DAY* when it really matters, the weather gods have decreed that all hell will be let loose.

And so, I prepare as best I can.

- ☑ Take plenty of old T-shirts to wear and throw away at the start line.
- ☑ Purchase a one-size-fits-all rain poncho from the marathon expo to wear on top of the five other insulating layers.
- ☑ Wear a pair of long compression socks underneath your winter mittens, accepting that your hands will be entirely numb and useless for the entire race.
- ☑ Place shower caps from the hotel bathroom over both trainers (two on each shoe).

I will soon discover that the shower cap shoe protectors are only effective for the first twenty metres as I walk across to the transportation buses which will take us to the start of the race. From that point on, they will become clogged up with mud from the short distance we have trudged across already sodden, boggy grass verges, and will be chewed up by tree roots. They are designed to be shower caps and they can't work miracles after all.

I'm hiding in the subway station just before forcing myself to go out into the lashing, icy rain. It's time to layer up. Everyone else is doing the same. We are all mentally preparing ourselves to venture out into the monsoon that awaits us, knowing that we will have hours to wait before the marathon begins. I am now a walking human clothes rail made up of:

- 1x skin-tight thermal upper body layer.
- 2x old T-shirts which I had intended to throw away at the start of the race. That is looking increasingly unlikely. One has been generously donated from a person who ran the Boston 5k race *in the sunshine* just two days before.
- 1x gilet which I would *never* usually dream of running anywhere – let alone a marathon – in.
- 1x $9.99 'Boston Strong' one-size-fits-all poncho which I purchased at the expo.
- 1x pair sodden shorts (there is no point in even trying to keep them dry).
- 1x pair compression socks which are now dirty grey in appearance. Previously, they were bright pink.
- 1x pair running shoes which can no longer be identified because they are now encased in …
- 2x shower caps in a desperate attempt to keep them – I can't even bring myself to say the word – dry.

I can see endless queues of yellow school buses, which remind me of *The Simpsons*, and row upon row of soggy runners waiting to board them for the journey to the start of the race. I stand behind a man who is simply staring at the ground, slowly shuffling forward. This feels completely surreal. I eventually board the bus and take a seat next to a meek-looking girl with nervous eyes. She smiles weakly; neither of us feel like talking. The bus finally pulls away and I think to myself that however long the journey to Hopkinton is, it will take me far, far longer to run back here. The bus meanders endlessly. Every time it slows down, my heart starts thumping loudly in my chest and I grab my bag preparing to stand up, but then it sets off again. *Bloody hell. How far away is the start?* All of a sudden, 26.2 miles feels like a hell of a long way.

Finally, the bus stops and there is a general wave of reluctance for anybody to move. I consider sliding down and hiding behind one of the seats, but on accepting that staying on the bus is not a viable option, survival mode kicks in. What can I do for the next two and a half hours to stay warm and dry – or at least prevent early onset hypothermia before the race even begins? I look across the road and I see my answer. A row of bright blue Portaloos. My plan is to hide out in one of these for as long as possible until I need to line up in my starting wave. No queues have formed just yet – it's still far too early – and so I should be able to protect myself inside the plastic shelter for as long as I need.

As I make my way to the Portaloos, I see runners picking up discarded, filthy clothing and putting it on. A woman is stepping gingerly into some cacky, oversized joggers; a man is struggling into a dirty-looking hoody which he has collected from the side of the road. I've never seen anything like it.

I arrive at my Portaloo and inside it's as clean as a whistle. I'm so relieved. The toilet roll is still in its wrapper and there is no piss on the floor or in the strongly sanitised urinal bowl.

I sit down and make myself at home. I have a clear plastic bag with me which is full of all the things I might need before and/or during the race. All of it will be discarded if I don't eat it/drink it/bin it/wear it while I'm running for 26.2 miles.

I begin to unpack my plastic bag. I place a banana, some gels and a caffeine shot on a small shelf to my right. My mitten gloves are already sodden and cold. I take them off and lay them out on the plastic surrounding the toilet seat in the hope that they will dry, but I know they won't. I have brought a spare pair of bright pink compression socks with me, thinking that these will make decent *extra* gloves to go inside my *actual* gloves. I wrestle my cold, wrinkly hands into the tight stockings and then again into my sodden inov-8 mittens. Now I can't do anything at all with my hands. I spend the next hour taking them off to move bits and pieces around on my plastic shelf and putting them back on again.

I am sitting in my new temporary home listening to the pouring rain as it hammers onto the plastic roofing, feeling pleased with myself for having the ingenuity to find some shelter from the relentless downpour outside these blue plastic walls. My mind has been drifting away, but I don't know where to. Likely anywhere but here.

I can hear muffled voices and loud, banging doors. What time is it? I have a terrifying thought that I may need to leave my Portaloo shelter and go to my starting pen. I know that I am in the second corral (a word I hadn't heard until now) and we have a starting time of 10.25 a.m. I look at my watch and it is already 9.30 a.m. *Shit!* I know we have to gather in our starting pens early – it's one of the few things I remember from the information booklet which I swiftly discarded.

I leave it as long as I dare and then I pack up my clear plastic bag (having removed and reassembled my hand-sock/wet-glove combo for the umpteenth time) and begrudgingly unlock the door. I don't want to step outside. I can see that long, bedraggled queues have begun to form. This is bad news, as there is no way I will be able to come back in here and hide again on the off-chance that I have another wait ahead of me.

I hear the final *slam* of my Portaloo door as it shuts behind me and I trudge past other drenched runners who are clothed head to foot in everything from boiler suits, pyjama bottoms and old jeans to ancient tracksuits and even long-forgotten Christmas jumpers. People have plastic bags over their feet and their shoulders, and some have shower caps on their heads and – like me – also on their feet. It is simply a case of who can keep driest for the longest. But we are all playing a losing game: everyone I see without exception is wet through to the bone and shivering like a frightened animal.

I snake my way amongst the walking jumble sale and eventually make it to the wall of volunteer race marshals who are guarding the entrance to the starting area. 'RED numbers ONLY!' are the irritated shouts coming from the barricade of individuals who are holding umbrellas and wearing Boston Marathon padded waterproof jackets – but they still look soaked to the bone and very, very cold. 'If you have a WHITE number on, you CANNOT COME IN HERE. RED NUMBERS ONLY!' The shouts are sounding increasingly frustrated with runners from other waves desperately trying to move beyond the holding area to the starting pens. Who can blame us?

I need to show my race number to a marshal gatekeeper. I glance down to my chest and struggle to peel away four wet layers. It takes some effort to locate my bib number through my hand-sock/wet-glove combo. *Shit! I HAVE A WHITE NUMBER.* They are still working their way through the first corral of runners, so I must wait my turn. I'm told that this will be in approximately twenty-five minutes, once the first wave has set off (their start time is 10 a.m.).

*Bollocks!*

There are now long, snaking queues at all of the Portaloos. I now join the back of one of the lines simply for something to do, somewhere to stand. I tuck myself in behind a young lad who is standing in the fewest clothes of anyone I have seen today. *What on earth is he thinking?* He is shivering like a malnourished, wet dog in a pair of tiny shorts and the thinnest cagoule which is so thoroughly saturated that it has formed a second skin, hugging his entirely fat-free body as though he has been vacuum-packed. This isn't right. He could become seriously ill. I can't simply stand here and do nothing. 'Here, take this spare top,' I say, reaching into my clear plastic bag and handing over the one remaining item of clothing I own which I am unable to wear. (I already have five saturated layers on. I figure that another one will not help.) 'Are you sure?' he says, looking at me disbelievingly with his big, brown, terrified eyes. I notice his hollow, sunken cheeks. A bearded man who is standing close by notices my gesture and hands the shivering boy two hand-warmers. It may be that we have just saved him from hypothermia before the marathon has even begun.

I take my turn in frequenting another Portaloo. This one is filled with the stench of nervous shits and piss which sloshes around the floor from where blokes have missed the urinal and women have opted against sitting on the toilet seat, preferring to hover in mid-air instead. No more than twenty-five seconds later, I am relieved to escape from the putrid fumes and back into the downpour as it continues to cascade from the furious skies.

I walk back up to the Race Marshal guardians at the marathon starting zone entry point. This time, all those wearing white numbers are permitted through into the waiting pens. This time, I don't need to check my bib number (which is still hidden under five layers of drenched clothes) to know that, yes, it is my time to go.

I head off, my trainers no longer making any attempt to dodge the large pools of water collecting in the road, and instead sloshing straight through them safe in the knowledge that another drop – or another million drops – of freezing, icy rainwater won't make any difference now.

The hardest marathon of my life is about to begin …

When I turned up to run my dream marathon in April 2018, all wet behind the ears – and, well, just wet everywhere – I could never have imagined that the conditions would be the worst in the race's 122-year history. What about those odds?! It happened at a time when everything else in my life was in absolute chaos and I honestly wondered if the torrential weather was simply a reflection of my inner struggle. I've read enough of those 'you bring your own reality into existence' spooky voodoo books. And so, at the time of writing in June 2021, I am putting it out into the universe that me and the Boston Marathon are not done.

I'm by no means the only person to have such a strong, unresolved feeling about a specific race – as though it needs to come full circle so that I can move on and close that chapter in my mind. The race becomes symbolic of something bigger than running. It is no longer just about the miles but about *everything else* we know we will have to endure and overcome to be back on the start line.

It is my goal to return to Hopkinton and make my way along the 26.2 miles via Routes 135, 16 and 30 to the famous yellow and blue finish line on Boylston Street.

Me and the Boston Marathon? We have unfinished business …

# JAMES

'It's a scorcher, isn't it?' he says as I sit down on the seat next to him, one of the few remaining on the bus.

It is August 2011 and we have just boarded the coach which will transport us to the start of the race – a half marathon across sand. I feel completely out of my depth. I have no idea how it feels to run even *one* mile on sand, let alone thirteen of them. I have no idea how the course has been marked out – how do you accurately measure a half marathon across a tidal bay? I'm aware of the importance of the tides and I feel some comfort in knowing that we have a reasonably large window in which we can do this without fear of being submerged by the sea, but that is really all I know. What I *do* know is that the midsummer heat is fierce. It may well be the hottest day of the year, and as I settle myself in for the forty-five-minute ride to the start of the race with my new friend, James, I can only pray for a coastal breeze once we step off this stifling coach.

The coach is packed full of runners and chatter. All kinds of advice is being proffered, whether it is required by the trapped recipient or not. 'Whatever you do, don't take Ibuprofen before the race,' I hear one old-timer say. 'It plays havoc with your stomach.'

Thankfully, James isn't one of the 'You don't want to do that' unwarranted-advice-offering crew. He sits quietly contemplating life while looking out of the window without forcing any conversation on to me.

I make some nervous quip about wearing zero sunblock and potential dehydration, and we settle into a comfortable silence on the packed bus as it sets off on its journey the long way around to the other side of

Morecambe Bay (it can't drive across the sand).

James is a quiet, reflective kind of chap. He doesn't start blurting out his running PBs or bombarding me with 'So, what energy gels do you use?' quickfire running banter. We're both a little reserved and understandably apprehensive ahead of today's race.

I presume from James's kit that he's no stranger to these kinds of things. He has a hydration vest with a full bladder in the back and I can see two water bottles poking out, plus handfuls of energy gels stuffed into either side. His long socks give him a 'serious runner' vibe, whereas I'm here in my non-branded ankle socks with my single 0.5-litre water bottle attached to my cheap running belt.

Time flies as the bus weaves along the coastal road to the start of the race. I learn snippets about James's life – about his family and work and how running is his 'thing'. He tells me that he likes to go on mini running adventures – it's how he chooses to take time out and escape from the daily grind.

We run together for the first few miles of the race in the unrelenting mid-day heat. The unusually late start time is one of the prerequisites to making sure that we don't become stranded several miles out at sea as the tide comes in and laps menacingly around our feet. The mass of people soon spreads out to become one long snake which is sidewinding its way across the sand. I look ahead and I can't see where it ends; I glance behind me and it's exactly the same. It's an extraordinary sight, this moving human sand creature which extends for many miles.

James is running along steadily beside me. We exchange a few words every now and again, like we're checking in with each other, before returning to the strangest sound: complete silence other than hundreds of feet hop-skipping and shuffling their way across a tidal bay. I make a mental note to remember this moment. There are no feet rhythmically tap-tapping on tarmac or cars beeping support as they drive past. There are no crowds standing alongside railings with jelly babies and plates of quartered oranges. This is the strangest – and possibly the most beautiful – sound I have ever heard. And it feels like being *a part of* something unique, not just standing by and observing it. I am one of the pairs of feet making their way steadily across the sand. James is here, too. Both of us are experiencing this unique race – a race we will never forget ...

It is June 2021 – almost exactly ten years since I sat next to James on the bus and we ran that half marathon together across Morecambe Bay. His face pops up on my computer screen – he looks exactly the same, only perhaps with more flecks of silver in his hair.

It feels completely surreal to be speaking to him again after all this time. We've kept in touch via social media, occasionally commenting on each other's posts, but we haven't spoken to each other in the many years since. A whole decade has passed, and we have both experienced plenty in that time. As soon as I hear his Wigan accent it takes me straight back to the summer of 2011 – right at the start of my own running journey and a time before James would find himself face to face with a cancer diagnosis.

I know fragments of James's story, but I want to know more. I ask him about his running journey and where it all began.

James has always been into his sports – mainly football – although he never saw himself as a runner. While chatting with one of the school mums one day, James found himself becoming intrigued by her marathon training. 'I was interested in the process of getting from A to B,' he tells me. 'I was fascinated by the journey of *how* to run a marathon.' Thirsty for more information, he set about finding out everything he could about the training required to run for 26.2 miles, and so the running seed was sown. James joined his friend Caroline on one of her long training runs, and although he couldn't walk the next day, he never looked back.

James secured a charity place for the London Marathon 2011 and the hard work began. But he would hit an early bump in the road. Just as his training was building up for the marathon, he tore his labrum (the ring of cartilage around his hip). 'I was told to stop running immediately and the consultant said that I wouldn't be able to run long distances again.' James remembers going into work the next day and being completely devastated because he realised how much he wanted to run that marathon.

James had a hip operation in December 2010, and began training again in the following February, giving himself just *two months* before standing on the start line of the London Marathon. Unbelievably, and against medical advice or any realistic expectation, he completed the marathon – the same marathon I ran which kick-started my new life as a runner, and a mother, and a person who was finally in control of her mental health.

The drama continued for James on his running journey when, within a year, the labrum in his *other* hip tore. His dreams of running his second (Manchester) marathon were over, and the following year was spent recovering from surgery on not one, but both hips. Time out was required. James needed to give his body time to recuperate and strengthen following the trauma of both hip operations.

2014 came around, by which time James had slowly regained his fitness. He had plans to run the Manchester Marathon in the April, but things would once again prove difficult. He came down with a nasty virus just a few days before the race, losing five pounds in weight and knowing that he wouldn't have recovered fully by the time he got to the start line. James turned up and ran anyway, but ten miles into the marathon he had to pull over, vomiting on the side of the road. 'It was really embarrassing because it looked like I wasn't fit or hadn't trained properly,' he says. 'I ran to the place where my mum and dad were waiting for me on the course, and I was just so poorly I had no choice but to pull out of the race. I was devastated.' All these years later and I can still sense the frustration and upset in James's voice.

James talks about being forced to make 'the walk of shame' to collect his bags from the start of the Manchester Marathon and my mind flips back to my own experience of the same. Being swept up in a St John's ambulance in full view of a thousand pairs of eyes in early 2017 is not a memory I particularly cherish, but we can at least laugh at the experience. It happens to us all – it's just part of the game.

I can feel the emotion surrounding this event for James all these years later, and I guess it's a reminder that running and racing can be an emotional rollercoaster at times. Along with the euphoric moments of personal victories and PBs come the heartbreaks and disappointments. I've experienced enough of those myself, but it's something that as runners we need to be prepared for. Stepping off a marathon course ten miles in is going to hurt; it's a sense of failure – of quitting when the going gets tough. It's a bruised ego and a failed negotiation with your body which you just can't win. But sometimes you *can't* just keep putting one foot in front of the other. Sometimes injuries or illness – anything from a stomach cramp to a persistent niggle – can steal your dreams from right in front of you. Even the conditions on the day are merciless. You weren't expecting to run 26.2 miles in lashing, icy rain and a Baltic headwind?* Oh, sorry about that. But those are the conditions you're faced with today (*Boston Marathon 2018). You didn't predict the freakish heatwave which would arrive precisely on the weekend of the London Marathon?† Bad luck. You'll just have to deal with it and do your best on the day (†London Marathon 2018 – although thankfully I couldn't run that day as I was still recovering from the monsoon in Boston).

The realisation that running can play with our emotions in such a dramatic way seems strange and slightly *unbalanced*. Why does it matter so much to us? What is it about running that brings with it euphoria and heartbreak in equal measure? I guess it's the yin and the yang – the balance in all things. To experience the runner's highs, we need to prepare ourselves to face the DNFs and the gutting lows. Is that a metaphor for life? Does knowing the grim alternative make the victories taste even sweeter? It is all part of the risk we take when we turn up to races – the risk of failing or falling short; the risk of humiliation – of knowing how close we are at any given moment to the wheels completely falling off and sobbing on the kerb with our head in our hands. Perhaps that is the allure of the marathon. The race where there is absolutely every opportunity for anything to happen – for the weather gods to trash our dreams or unavoidable stomach cramps to stop us in our tracks. In truth, we can train as hard as we like. We can stick to a plan and put in the miles, but then things can happen on the day that are completely outside our control. It's a risk we take and a negotiation in which we have precious little bargaining power. Perhaps there is something healthy in this keeping our egos in check. Ultimately, we are at the whim of the marathon gods, no matter how much preparation we make.

James and I talk about the cocktail of emotions around the build-up to running a marathon and the rollercoaster ride that is inevitably part of the journey to get there.

So far in his story, he has run two marathons – one completed, one aborted through illness – and he has suffered two broken hips with accompanying operations.

James tells me that he is a person who needs to complete things – tasks, goals, journeys, whatever. He needs to come full circle and see things through to the end, or at least until he feels as though they are fully resolved in his own mind. I've seen evidence of this in his story with the Manchester Marathon – both times being hampered by either injury or illness and a feeling of unfinished business looming over him. In truth, he will never be satisfied until he can tick the box that says 'job done' about any task that he has undertaken. I recognise this quality in myself. Is that a common experience for those of us who choose to put ourselves on the start line of a race? Is that part of the unspoken deal with ourselves – that we have committed to seeing it through, come hell or high water? When we sign up for these things, are the seeds already sown that won't allow us to be satisfied with an unresolved outcome, like a DNF or a list of potential excuses for why it didn't work out for us on the day?

The next part of James's running journey happened alone and in complete silence. Struggling to know how his body might cope, he undertook to train for the Chester Marathon and ran it completely under the radar. 'I didn't tell anybody I was doing it,' he says. 'I went along by myself and started with the people in fancy dress right at the back.' James ran a personal best time and achieved his first sub-four-hour marathon on that day, and I can sense the delight and sheer joy as he describes that moment to me, almost as though this was restitution for all the prior disappointments. I can tell how much it means to him – the emotion is still there in his voice as he recalls that moment, a time when the stars aligned and made up for the obstacles that had gone before. This one was personal: James versus all the challenges that he'd already had to overcome.

'Some things in my life I need to do on my own,' he says, reflecting for a moment.

We talk for a while about the need for many of us to do this – as though there are certain times when the battle we are fighting feels very personal. Sometimes it is just you and the goal ahead. It is a thing that only you alone can endure. I know that feeling so well – as though there is a place deep inside of us that only we can access. It's a place we don't even visit ourselves very often, but at times we need to go there to remind ourselves who we really are. Is it in the deepest part of our soul? Like a locked vault which only running can open? When it hurts so much and there is nowhere else to go but to dig deep inside your own spirit and access the oldest part of your DNA that instinctively knows how to survive. There is perhaps something about proving to ourselves that we can overcome, that we can endure.

Following his marathon success, James set his sights on a different objective. 'I absolutely love mountains and trails and I heard about the Keswick Ultra 50k,' he tells me. He then set himself the challenge of completing the race with a friend. Sensibly, their only goal was to finish, and James and his friend crossed the line together. 'There was no medal, so I made myself a cardboard one,' he says. I laugh out loud, having done exactly the same thing with my daughter. This was a beautiful race for James: the fantastic scenery, running with his friend and finishing his very first ultramarathon – it was a truly great experience. Sadly though, the high wouldn't last for very long.

James couldn't understand why he felt so unbelievably tired. I know what you're thinking: *he'd just run an ultramarathon!* Logic would surely accept that as an explanation. James put his immense fatigue and weight loss down to that glaringly obvious factor, together with increased stress at work, but something just didn't feel right. Going into the race, he felt absolutely exhausted. On finishing it, even more so.

Two weeks later, James was in the shower one morning when he noticed that one of his testicles felt slightly larger than normal. He mentioned it to his wife, Vicky, and she told him to get it checked out immediately. He took her advice but says that he didn't think anything more about it. Following an initial appointment with his GP, he went out walking his dog. It was just another day. 'They phoned me whilst I was out with the dog and asked me if I could come back in the next day,' he recalls. 'I had a feeling then that something was amiss.' James's wife works in the NHS and, with this news, she was on high alert. The following day, James and Vicky went along to their GP. 'He just sat me down straight away and said, "James, you've got testicular cancer" and that was it.'

There's something stunning about the matter-of-factness of James receiving this news, and the way that these emotionally devastating word-bombs brought his life crashing down within a matter of moments. But isn't that the reality of life? The same was true for Carly with her two breast cancer diagnoses; the same was true for Lars-Christian with the death of his newborn daughter and for Lisa with the news of her mother's devastating fall. News like this can't be avoided; it is devastating however it arrives.

I find myself momentarily lost for words, like I am vicariously experiencing a similar sense of shock. 'What do you do with that?' I ask him, as though there is any kind of a simple or straightforward answer that he can give me. 'It really knocked me,' he says. 'I considered myself healthy; I thought I was strong. I'd just completed an ultramarathon, for goodness' sake! It hit me like a bullet.'

Things happened so quickly that James barely had time to process anything. From first noticing his swollen testicle to receiving the cancer diagnosis, his life suddenly picked up a sense of urgency. He was on fast-forward. 'My first thoughts were for the others – for my wife and kids,' he says, having to swallow the lump in his throat. I notice the wobble in his voice and the way his eyes look away from the screen as though he is accessing a very private, sacred place. 'I just wanted to do whatever I could to get fixed.'

James immediately went into fight mode. 'It was really hard telling my mum and dad,' he says, his voice quavering. 'They come from a generation where the word "cancer" is immediately associated with a death sentence, and I knew they would hear the news and think of it in that way.'

Explaining to his elderly parents that he wasn't necessarily going to die from his cancer was emotionally challenging for James. We discuss the generational attitude and fear towards cancer and the fact that our parents grew up in a world where cancer diagnosis and treatment was a far cry from the advances in medicine and technology we have the benefit of today.

Within just five days of his diagnosis, James was scheduled for an operation to remove the tumour. It was necessary to explore other areas of his body to make sure that the cancer hadn't spread. James was incredibly lucky. He caught his cancer in the early stages, but that doesn't take away the shock of a healthy, active and incredibly fit man receiving a cancer diagnosis in the first place.

James is the second person I have spoken to who has been diagnosed with early-stage cancer and has received successful treatment. Incredibly, he says, 'I still feel like a fraud at times.' Carly felt exactly the same way, as though her cancer wasn't devastating or serious enough to be actually classified as the 'C'-word. But how is that possible when considering all the utter devastation that comes along with a cancer diagnosis, including the mental health impact in those cases like James's that are caught and treated early? What about the trauma that isn't caused directly by the multiplying cancerous cells, but by the resounding effect on every other aspect of a person's life? What about absorbing the terror of family members – including frightened children and elderly parents? What about the ominous fear of the cancer returning, and an overwhelming sense of an 'invisible enemy' lurking somewhere in the body, ready to strike at any given moment? What about living in constant fear of a lump or bump being synonymous with a life-threatening illness? Following my discussions with James and Carly, I realise that there is *never* the option to go back to a time before, when cancer was something that happened to other people. Speaking to James and Carly, it is clear to me that the mental health impact of a cancer diagnosis is enormous at *whatever* stage it is diagnosed. 'You can repair yourself physically, but it's not as easy to recover mentally,' James says. 'I was a bit of a mess, to be honest.'

I have no personal experience of cancer. I can only imagine the tumult of emotions a person experiences following a cancer diagnosis of any kind. James explains how he found it difficult to talk to anybody about it. 'I just don't really talk about my feelings,' he says in his broad Wigan accent. I get it. We've all heard the mental health slogan 'It's good to talk', and, thankfully, open discussion around mental health is encouraged far more than used to be the case. But for some individuals – men in particular – doing this can be much harder than it sounds. James fits into this category. He is not a man who has grown up learning that it's healthy for him to talk about his feelings, or perhaps even knowing how to do that.

James eventually went back to work, but he struggled to focus. He was foggy-headed and describes occasions when he would sit with his head in his hands and feel nothing but complete despair. 'My bosses at work did everything they could,' he says. In one of his professional development review meetings, he opened up and said that he couldn't understand why he felt so low, or why he couldn't shake himself out of it. James was fortunate in that his boss immediately arranged for him to receive some counselling. 'The fact that my counsellor was herself a cancer survivor made it incredibly helpful for me because I knew that she understood what I was going through,' he says.

Thank goodness James felt able to be honest with his boss and, in turn, his employer saw the need for him to receive some specialist support in dealing with the mental health aspect of his cancer diagnosis, even when his physical treatment had been successful. It's fantastic to hear how beneficial James found his counselling sessions. For a quiet, self-contained person who is more familiar with keeping things to himself and 'sucking it up', the opportunity to talk openly to a qualified person about his experiences came at the right time and offered James the release he so desperately needed from his own trapped thoughts. He needed to open a valve and allow all the built-up fear and trauma of his cancer diagnosis out.

Around a year later, James was back running again. One day, while out on his usual run, he noticed a strange mark on his arm which he tells me appeared to glow oddly in the sunlight. He mentioned it at his next check-up (he was still having regular appointments with his oncologist following his testicular cancer) and the doctor looked at the mark on his skin and found another similar one on his back. James was diagnosed with skin cancer.

This time, I don't have any words.

'It was only in the very early stages, and was simply removed,' he says. No further treatment was necessary. James says that he dodged another bullet but the impact on him mentally was completely devastating, and I can understand why. He tells me that he felt as though cancer could creep up on him anywhere, at any time, and in any place on his body. The fact that he had experienced no symptoms whatsoever and that it was by sheer luck that this skin cancer had been spotted made it even worse – rather like his health was a game of chance, like rolling dice. I can imagine how that might play awful games with a person's head. It would be so easy to question every possible sign – a mole you hadn't previously noticed – as a potential threat. *'Is this blemish new? Have I always had a mark here?'* Speaking to James, I am beginning to realise that when cancer rears its ugly head, that is bad enough. When the enemy is creeping around your body silently and hiding away in the corners, out of sight like a ninja, that must be a terrifying feeling. The 'not knowing' affected James badly and played with his head constantly. How do you fight an enemy that you can't even see?

James trusted his oncologist when he was told that his skin cancer was completely removed and that no further treatment was necessary, but as James says in his typical, no-nonsense way, 'The truth of the matter is that once you've had cancer, then you live in fear for the rest of your life.' At least this is James's own experience. But on the positive side, it also means that he is now in the best position to be able to identify any future warning signs, of being fast-tracked for any necessary treatment, and he is already on the radar of the medical professionals whose job it is to help him to remain cancer-free.

The word 'fear' crops up many times during our conversation. It's a horrible word. James explains that most of the time it fades into the background. Over the five years of check-ups following his testicular cancer diagnosis, James's confidence began to grow with every medical check confirming that his body was now clear and the cancer hadn't returned.

In 2018, James did several races for Cancer Research, but he had a bigger goal in mind. He wanted to go back and run the Keswick Ultra 50k – the same race he had completed just weeks before his first dreadful cancer diagnosis. I ask why it was so important for him to go back and run that race again, because I can sense that this was incredibly personal. 'I needed to come full circle and to run it as a way of saying to myself, "I'm well again",' he says. Running the Keswick Ultra 50k was James's way of demonstrating that he'd beaten the cancer. When he stood on the start line of that race five years before, the cancer had been there in his body, hiding in the shadows. Now, as he stood on the start line once again, he had lived with cancer, and he had survived. That is why James needed to put himself back in that particular race and make it across the finish line. It was about his solo journey as a cancer survivor rather than a cancer victim. This time, he would cross the finish line entirely cancer-free.

James's journey is now complete. Although he is constantly setting himself new adventures, he's never felt as though he needs to do the Keswick mountain race again.

Since sharing his story with me, James tells me that he is *still* determined to beat his nemesis, the Manchester Marathon. 'I've had two attempts and each of them has been scuppered by injury or illness. For me, it's like having unfinished business. That medal will be mine!' Interestingly, James mixes up his training nowadays. 'It's not just about running for me,' he says. 'I go to the gym; I enjoy spinning and swimming. I like to cross-train – it makes things feel more balanced and more interesting!'

# LIZ

Sometimes you get a strong feeling that you have a lot in common with a person. It can happen almost instantly, without having any idea why you feel that way. This is exactly what happened with Liz. I guess we have certain obvious commonalities. We're both forty-three years old (our birthdays are within weeks of each other); we both come from Yorkshire; we're both not-quite-naturally blonde; we're both very funny indeed. These things unite us. But beyond those things, we both share a deep love of running and both of us have experienced first-hand how running came to help us at a time when our lives careered off track and hit the proverbial fan. Furthermore, not only did running save us at a critical time in our lives, but we both performed at our very best when our personal circumstances were arguably at their most challenging.

My call with Liz feels like I'm chatting with a good mate. Which is ideal, because this Zoom call will be subject to no less than *four* technical failures. Each time, we will have to abruptly stop recording and clumsily connect back up again when the 1990s dial-up internet connection we are apparently using decides to crank into action. We laugh about the fact that I won't have one interview to listen to on playback; I will have four of them. It's a good job I feel like I know Liz so well already …

Liz tells me that she first started running in her late twenties with a few friends from work. They would go out a couple of times a week and run along the canal. 'It was nothing serious and I was absolutely rubbish,' she says. 'It was just something to get us out of the office for an hour or so.' The running stopped when Liz fell pregnant with her daughter, and she didn't pick up her trainers again until after her son was born a few years later. 'I knew I needed to do something to feel like myself again,' she says. Liz believes that running helped her to rediscover her identity, which she felt she had lost in the tangle of motherhood. Many of the women I've spoken to have felt exactly the same way. We lose a part of ourselves through the journey to motherhood – even if it is only a tiny part. And we do that knowingly and willingly, because our bodies become mobile incubators for a period of nine months, and the effects of that continue thereafter. Going through that process twice in short succession meant that Liz felt a double whammy of post-natal overwhelm, and this was a large part of her motivation to run again.

Liz has asthma, and she recalls her first outings following her return to running. 'I could barely run for half a mile without wanting to die,' she laughs. Regardless, she kept putting her trainers on and gradually she began to set herself goals: 5k soon became 10k, which led to a half marathon, and ultimately she set her sights on running a marathon. Liz was offered a charity place to run in the 2014 Paris Marathon. To help her realise that dream, she joined a local running club at the end of 2013, and she says this was the point at which her real love of running began. 'I remember turning up to the running club for the very first time and seeing people standing in little huddles, wondering if I would ever fit in and make friends.'

Liz had no idea at the time how important this step would be. Not only would the running club prove to be a vital source of strength for her during the months of marathon training ahead, but the support and friendship from within the club would also prove to be pivotal for her mental health at a time of personal crisis.

None of us knows what is waiting around the corner, and it's a blooming good job we don't, because some stuff is just too shitty to comprehend. Without even realising it, Liz was building the foundations for when her life would fall apart. She was meeting the people who would be there and who would support her through some of the worst times of her life. Perhaps intuitively, she already knew that she was meeting her tribe.

And so, Liz began training for her very first marathon. It's a daunting task for anyone, but with the help of the other runners in the club, she soon began to clock up the miles. This is where Liz and I differ. She planned for her first marathon in a far smarter way than I did, the botched basis of my own marathon training plan being detailed in the pages of my first book. Unlike me, Liz placed herself amongst people who knew a thing or two about running marathons. Many were old hands with multiple marathons under their belts who were happy to share their experience and knowledge with the newbies, including Liz.

The Paris Marathon was a great experience for Liz. She enjoyed both training with the club and the race itself, although without having any idea of a predicted time, she found herself setting off with the running rhinos at the back of the pack. Regardless, Liz finished her first marathon in a very respectable four hours and seven minutes. And we all know that the first marathon is simply about finishing it. None of us knows what to expect. However, this gave Liz a benchmark – and it was a higher benchmark than mine (I finished my first London Marathon in four hours and twenty-five minutes). Liz had a far better plan, and it paid off. With her first marathon done, she had already come a long way since putting on her running shoes and reclaiming her sense of self following the onset of motherhood.

At the beginning of 2016, Liz and her family experienced a terrible shock when her younger brother suffered a serious mental health breakdown. While he was receiving treatment in a centre close to Liz's family home, she visited him almost every day. 'I was consumed with worry and most of my headspace was completely taken up with his recovery,' she says. 'In addition to that, much of my time was spent visiting him in hospital.'

Suddenly, everything changed. Liz's attention was taken away from her normal, everyday life and her energy was spent tending to the family emergency which had just presented itself without notice. Everything was affected, including Liz's relationship. 'I wasn't sleeping or eating properly,' she tells me, 'and I guess other things took a back seat because I just didn't have the capacity to deal with much else on top of my brother's recovery.'

We know this happens. Life events throw us off course and the result can be catastrophic on those closest to us. Liz is incredibly honest in admitting how this stress manifested in her marriage. Of course it did – she would be inhuman otherwise! But the damage was much greater than it might have been reasonable to anticipate. Later that year, Liz discovered that her husband had been having an affair. She experienced every possible emotion on that day. Suddenly, she was confronted with the reality of all the tiny clues she had tried so hard to ignore in the many months that had come before: her husband being distant and strangely cold towards her; a general feeling of being unloved; something not feeling quite right which she was unable to put her finger on. She now had her answer.

To be clear, Liz isn't sharing this story so that she can take great joy in finger-pointing at her ex-husband, who is the father of her two children. She doesn't come across as being some moral crusader who takes no responsibility whatsoever for the failings in her first marriage; not at all. She is simply describing a melting pot of emotional pressure. Liz found herself in a situation where every conceivable way she turned in her life, there was stress piled on top of more stress. She needed to be able to function in her daily life; she still needed to get the kids up and make them some breakfast; she needed to take them to school. She needed to go to work and carry out her job without falling apart. She needed to visit her brother and support him in his mental health recovery. Unbelievably, Liz still needed to go back home with her children every single day and live under the same roof as the man she had married who had told her that he didn't love her any more and didn't want to work on their relationship. And she needed to wake up every single day and go through it all again.

Anyone who has been through a relationship break-up will know the emotional toll it takes, regardless of any 'rights' or 'wrongs'. It is the death of a union, the end of a partnership. Something which once was beautiful (or mostly) has turned sour and hateful, and as the fog descends it becomes harder and harder to see any of the shiny parts. It's like being submerged in a vat of pain and not knowing how to get out. The walls close in on themselves and an idyllic family home can suddenly feel more like a prison with no air. And that's without even mentioning the children. We know they pick up on all the subtle (and not-so-subtle) messages flying around. They see the tear-stained cheeks and the smudged mascara. They know why they've been told to go to their room ... again: it's code for 'more shouty voices and nasty words'. Of course, we try to protect them from the worst of it, but kids aren't stupid. They see everything. Even the painful silences between the words. They hear those, too. They know what that is.

And so, unsurprisingly, Liz was on the verge of going under. Her mental health was at breaking point.

Enter stage left: running.

Liz's running club take part in a series of VETS cross-country races every year. She noticed that during this particular year, her finishing times and positions were extraordinarily good compared to the year before. 'I just channelled all my anger and frustration into my running,' she says. 'Running was a vent; it was somewhere for it to all come pouring out.'

I can relate so strongly to Liz's experience. The year 2014 was the same for me. This was the year when I left a relationship that had been holding me back, and for the first time in a long time I felt like I was flying when I ran. All the built-up emotions of the years that had gone before and a sense of newfound freedom added up to more PBs than I could keep up with – including my marathon PB which still stands (three hours and sixteen minutes).

Liz was also finding her inner warrior by putting on her running shoes. She was building back the strength that was eroded when one of the main pillars of her life was suddenly smashed to pieces. Running was Liz's way of reminding herself just how strong she was, and how strong she could be in her future life – whatever it looked like.

People at the running club began to notice the dramatic improvement in Liz's running, and although some people close to her knew about her personal circumstances, it was becoming very clear that she had discovered her very own rocket fuel. There is often a great emphasis on progression within the running community, but I'm not sure that Liz's personal jet pack is the type that many people would want for themselves. 'It felt like a fire had been lit underneath me,' Liz says. 'I took all that negative energy and channelled it into my running.'

We discuss how incredible it is that we have both been on different journeys and yet we have shared the same experience. Running has been our rocket fuel, our therapy and our freedom following the break-up of a relationship. We have both run through the 'How on earth … ?' and

'What will happen?' unanswerable questions. We have both exhausted ourselves pounding up hills in the face of a future which suddenly feels uncertain; but at the top of the hill, we realise we can make it. Perhaps that's the thing. When you run and it hurts and you want to stop but you find a way to keep going, you are demonstrating your own strength. It's a bit like coaching yourself into self-belief. You move past the pain and the fear of 'what-ifs' and far beyond the point of despair. You keep moving forward because *that's what we all must do*. Simply that: keep taking steps forward. It reminds us that in life, moving forward is what we need to do.

And there is something about the need to physically rid ourselves of the negativity and the fear. I'm certainly no yogi, but I do believe in a strong mind–body connection. One impacts on the other: mental struggles can manifest themselves physically, and physical illness can morph into mental health challenges. 'I still look back on that part of my life and wonder how on earth I managed to get through it,' Liz says. 'I can't believe all that I achieved [through running] during the worst time in my life.'

Well, I can believe it.

Running therapy for me and Liz happened in three ways. Firstly, we ran by ourselves. Liz describes this as being a 'head clearer'. It's true! Being so focused on your breathing, the beauty around you and the sound of your own footsteps is a great way to allow any worries to simply melt away. It brings you back into the present. Thoughts may come and go, but in my experience, I find it easier for them to drift along while I'm running, instead of becoming stuck on a particular issue for which I don't yet have an answer.

Secondly, Liz found that running with a group helped her to process some of the pain of her experience and it made her realise that she wasn't alone: others had gone through similar things. 'I would run and chat with people from the club and they would tell me about their experiences,' Liz says. 'It was cathartic and a huge release for me to talk to people who were supporting me along the way.'

Thirdly, we both ran races. Lots of them. It was a chance for us to blast through the anxiety that otherwise threatened to hang around us like an unwelcome fog. Racing was a chance for us to prove to ourselves just what we were capable of. Can I hold this pace for 13.1 or 26.2 miles? Can I maintain this tempo right to the end? Liz experienced this during her year of adversity. She began to kick ass at her running club's cross-country season, storming her way to third place. Mine was mainly half-marathon distances, and I ran two marathons during 2014 – my year of liberation – where I smashed my personal best times to pieces. 'The year I got my divorce papers through was the same year I achieved my marathon PB,' Liz says, laughing. Because what else can you do? She had been hoping to achieve a Good for Age time in the 2017 Manchester Marathon, which for Liz was three hours and forty-five minutes. But on that day, she stormed through the finish line in three hours and twenty-four minutes, a whopping twenty-plus minutes clear of her goal.

Both of us had breakthrough running years at the worst times in our lives. Surely there is something to be taken from the fact that this was possible – not when everything was working in our favour, but at the very opposite end of the scale. Our adversity fuelled us in a way that perfect conditions couldn't.

I ask Liz how she felt following her breakthrough running year. I know that for me, it felt like I was Charlie Bucket blasting up through the great glass elevator. To realise that the limits you once put on yourself no longer exist can be both exhilarating and scary at the same time. You have unleashed your own hidden power. It means that your comfort zone no longer exists. You are forced to adjust and reset your boundaries because – well, they have now been reset for you. There is a sense of glancing around wondering, 'What just happened?' And it's funny how we both experienced these Charlie Bucket glass ceiling moments at a time in our lives when we really needed to believe in ourselves again. We needed that feeling of strength; we needed reminding that it was already within us. And it happened right when it mattered the most. Not so that we could revel in some gloating ego-trip amongst members of our respective running clubs, but so that we could know deep inside that we had the strength to get through the most challenging times in our lives. That's why these breakthrough moments were transformational for me and Liz.

Unbelievably, Liz had to endure living with her ex-husband, knowing that their marriage was over while 'keeping face' with their children for *over a year!* A whole year of living under a roof of anger, resentment, deep sadness and lies. That is a feat of endurance in itself. Perhaps Liz's breakthrough marathon was simply a reminder that she could hold on. She could stick it out for as long as it took to get through to her own finish line – the marathon she had already been running for well over a year.

Liz has come a long way in the years since. 'I just don't know what I would have done without running,' she says. 'I honestly think I would have fallen apart. It's incredible to think of all the amazing friendships I've made and the incredible support network I now have.'

Since sharing her story with me, Liz has enjoyed being able to run once again with her friends from the running club since the lifting of Covid restrictions. 'Running with my club again this summer was really special,' she says, explaining how difficult she has found not being able to do that over lockdown. What does running hold for Liz now? 'Losing my dad in 2018 has really changed my outlook on running,' she says. After all that she has endured, Liz explains that she feels like she has achieved everything she could have dreamt of, and so she is happy to simply enjoy running and not think about chasing any PBs for now.

# ENOUGH

There are inherent dangers in being the type of person who asks – or more likely *demands* – an enormous amount of themselves. Somebody who believes they must try harder, do more, be better. Otherwise known as 'A Perfectionist'. Not of others – they have different, more reasonable rules to play by, and we would *never* expect anybody else to meet our own exacting standards. The perfectionist sees only one variable in any given set of circumstances. There is only one person to blame when things don't work out ... and we all know who that is: *the buck stops here ...*

Of course, things don't always work out as you'd hope. You set yourself goals, but sometimes life places unforeseen obstacles in the way, making the realisation of that goal simply unfeasible. You just have to suck it up. A rational, logical person might console themselves with the thought that 'it's a shame it didn't go my way' for whatever reason. But what happens when a perfectionist turns inwards and blames themselves for a series of events which are completely outside their control? Running the Dubai Marathon in 2016 taught me that *I am that person*. I am the one who turned inwards, berating myself when my own ridiculously high expectations were not met.

My marathon begins in the hotel bedroom at around 11 p.m. Dubai time. I'm hopelessly unable to sleep. It's fast approaching 7 p.m. back in the UK and my body clock is still in that time zone, instinctively wanting to reach for a beer and to nibble on a bowl of salt and vinegar crinkle-cuts. I'm nowhere near ready to switch off for the night. But I have a 4 a.m. wake-up call looming, so I have no choice but to try and get a few hours' sleep. I shuffle around in the dark repositioning pillows until I finally admit defeat and switch the lights back on. I eat a small snack and pretend to read my book until just after midnight. Eventually, I manage to doze off, but even while I'm purportedly asleep, my mind is fully alert.

My marathon has already begun.

The offensive *harp* alarm notification rouses me from my semi-slumber at 4 a.m. It should wake me gently, but instead I leap out of bed like I've been connected to jump leads. Adrenaline is already coursing through my veins – that and sheer panic. Breakfast arrives right on time – but it's 4.15 a.m. and miniature Danish pastries are about the last thing I feel like tucking into at this ungodly hour. Once my mini croissants have been consumed, I speed-change into my race gear, pack up my bags and do one final kit check before heading off for the 5 a.m. taxi.

The highways of Dubai are completely deserted. There is something strange in knowing that I'm about to embark on a marathon adventure while most of the city still sleeps. Arriving at the taxi drop-off point in the pitch black feels unworldly, like leaving home for some unthinkable emergency in the middle of the night. It's a novelty seeing Dubai's diamanté street decorations dazzling along the central reservations, but I'd expect nothing less out here, in Bling City.

I drop my bag at the luggage station and head to the start of the marathon. Mercifully, there's no time to dwell on what is to come. By the time I'm settled in the starting area, it's time for the off. They do things on time around here. Like clockwork, in fact.

The marathon begins in the dark – at 6.30 a.m. precisely – and the sun will rise shortly afterwards. Standing in the eerie darkness with sunglasses poised on my head, waiting for the punishing red ball to rise over the desert, feels odd. It is organised this way to delay tens of thousands of us marathon runners from baking in the scorching sun for as long as possible. I won't know what running in that kind of heat will feel like until there is no escape from it.

I set off at a reasonable pace, wanting to make sure that I don't push myself too hard too soon. I've coached myself into hopefully avoiding my usual marathon trappings of flying off too fast and burning out with a (very) long way to go. As I turn the first corner, I can see other runners approaching behind me on the other side of the highway. So far, so good. I am in control. But then again, I should be – I'm only four miles in! I am sticking to my 'comfortable early pace' race plan, and although I'm not unduly worried, I don't exactly feel great, either. My legs feel heavy, and I have an inkling that this will be a particularly long day. Still, I just about manage to maintain my seven-and-a-half-minute-mile pace for the first half of the race.

My perfectionist alter-ego head begins chuntering.

*'You SHOULD be able to maintain this pace, Rachel … '*

*'You've run marathons much faster than this, Rachel.'*

*'Don't even THINK about slowing down now, Rachel.'*

*'You should be doing BETTER THAN THIS, Rachel.'*

I find it difficult to process the conflicting messages I am receiving from my body and my mind. Physically, I am entering the pain cave far sooner than I would have liked. It's becoming harder and harder for me to maintain my target pace as my legs become increasingly leaden. I am also dropping off the small group I've been running with, and tellingly, I choose not to try and stay with them. I am falling behind. The cruel perfectionist taunts continue.

*'What's wrong with you, Rachel? Why can't you keep up?'*

*'How can THEY keep going at that pace, but YOU can't?'*

*'You should be doing better than this, Rachel.'*

*'Try harder, Rachel.'*

I begin talking to myself, trying to drown out the nasty jibes coming from my perfectionist alter ego. I play tricks in my head – breaking down the remaining miles into more manageable stages. Miles fourteen to seventeen – that's only one Parkrun. Then another Parkrun to reach twenty miles … and I break up the remaining six miles into two more Parkrun chunks. I don't know if it's helping, but I decide to tackle just one Parkrun at a time. When one is done, move on to the next.

Around mile seventeen, we turn a corner (there are precious few corners on the Dubai marathon route) and the tarmac feels like it's melting underneath my feet. There isn't a change of scenery. I look across at the runners who are a good few miles behind me as they are approaching the bend. I briefly scan their pained faces, but I am the one who is now entering the damage-limitation zone for my own marathon. I am in hanging-on territory, only it is happening far earlier in the race than I'd anticipated. My head spins with worry, heat and fatigue. *What the hell am I going to do?*

I can feel it slipping away. My legs increase in density with every step, and I can't help becoming frustrated. My perfectionist alter ego is right! *They should know what to do on a flat, straight marathon course, FFS!* And with the thousands of running miles I've already accumulated, they should surely assume a default position, which is to continue running at a certain pace until I say stop. Nothing more complicated than that. I don't think I'm being unreasonable. Well, my alter ego certainly doesn't. My mind is like a jockey frustratingly whipping his racehorse, but my body is feeling the repeated slash of the leather against swollen, scorched skin – and it really fucking hurts. I need an energy gel and a drink. Any excuse to briefly pull over and have a word with myself. *Come on, Rach. Think. Think of some way to get through this.* I set off running again, remembering my plan is to deal with five-kilometre Parkrun chunks one at a time and not to worry about the next one until I am in it. *Okay – it's a deal. I can do that.*

It hasn't really dawned on me that we are now running in the Arabian heat, which has crept up on us like a stealthy Dickensian pickpocket. I am careful to take in at least a small sip of water at every available drink station. I am doing well on that front – I'm managing to take on board regular carbohydrate gels and some liquid with electrolyte solution to replace the essential salts which I am losing by the bucketload. But no matter what I do, I feel like I'm losing grip of my pace. According to my running watch, I've just passed twenty miles. It doesn't help that all the road markers are in kilometres. I know rationally that my frustration is disproportionate, but I can't help it. I soon realise that obsessively staring at my watch doesn't make me run any faster. It just makes me worry and blame myself more. And I'm feeling dizzy.

I have six miles left to run, and I am a car with the red warning lights flashing: I have square wheels, my fuel tank is empty and I am leaking oil.

At any moment, I could just grind to a complete standstill. I want to stop running so badly it is almost compelling. It is a *NEED*. Something I *MUST DO*. I've no idea how, but I manage to dismiss it as a very bad idea, because I know that if I stop running – even for the shortest time – my legs won't start again. The chances are they wouldn't move another inch. It's a risk not worth taking. I just want this to finish. I need to get to the end, and for it to be over. With my burning desire to sit down on the molten tarmac at the side of the road quashed, I attempt to straighten my head out once again. When options are taken away, it helps to regain clarity. My *only* option is to keep on running. I decide to focus on that and nothing else.

The last two miles are wretched. I know then without any doubt that I am way outside my marathon PB of three hours and sixteen minutes. It just won't happen today. *But why not?* My alter ego taunts me. '*Why couldn't you make it happen today, Rachel? What's wrong with you? You SHOULD have made it happen. You should have got a PB today, Rachel, but you didn't. And that is all on YOU.*'

I squirm about on hearing his scathing judgement of my pathetic efforts. I wrestle back some rational thought – enough to readjust my expectations. *Could I be reasonably satisfied with a 3:30 marathon?* As disappointed as I would be, I tell myself that is still a very respectable marathon time, and I would at least be able to say that I couldn't have done any more today. Nothing at all. '*But it isn't a good marathon time FOR YOU, Rachel,*' my chimp interjects. I try to remain logical and focus on the positives instead of listening to my internal perfectionist mantra constantly berating me for '*not running well enough*'.

I grit my teeth, exhaust every ounce of willpower I can muster, and eventually cross the finish line in three hours and thirty-four minutes, my legs giving way underneath me* as I finally press 'stop' on my running watch (*I subsequently learn that this can be one effect of running in heat). I slump down at the side of the road a little way beyond the finish line, and I sob. I heave in exhausted breaths while fat, swollen tears streak down my salty face. I'm broken. Physically, I've given my all. But mentally, this marathon has hurt me even more.

The story should end here. I *should* tell you about limping back to the hotel resort after the marathon and consuming my bodyweight in high-quality protein cooked in exotic ways while sipping on pina coladas and staying completely immobile – just occasionally venturing from my sunlounger to the pool as a brief respite from the scorching heat. Sadly, that is not the story I can tell you. You see, the perfectionist alter-ego voice damaged me more than the marathon itself did on that day. I listened to his judgement and absorbed his words as though they were a reluctant truth I didn't want to hear. *'You just didn't try hard enough, Rachel. You were the only relevant variable, and on the day, you fell short.'* Forget about the scorching desert heat and the sleepless night. Pay no regard to the jet lag or your stalled body clock which presumed it was time for *Ant & Dec's Saturday Night Takeaway* rather than some ungodly hour approaching midnight. *The buck stops with you …*

The next morning, I wake in my hotel room and the taunts continue. My head spins with fatigue while my leg muscles scream with aches, every single movement forcing me to wince in pain. *Oh, no.* I can hear a voice. It's my perfectionist alter ego again. *Bloody hell – is he still going? Hasn't he quit?*

No. He hasn't.

*'You failed yesterday, Rachel. You fell short of the goal. You are entirely responsible. There is no one else to blame. You MUST remedy this. You MUST try harder. This is NOT good enough. Do you hear me? THIS IS NOT ACCEPTABLE.'*

It feels like I'm being admonished by a disappointed teacher. I feel too numb to even cry. I look over at my trainers, which are still caked in dry, desert dust from the 26.2 miles they ran along the melting tarmacked highways a matter of hours before. I feel compelled towards them like a crack addict needing 'just one more hit'. *'You need to run again,'* my perfectionist alter ego advises me. *'You weren't good enough yesterday, and so you need to get out again and run today. Train harder. Do better. GO NOW. DO IT. RUN!'*

I drag myself over to my trainers. I hate myself for doing it, staring at them scornfully as though they are directly responsible for causing me so much pain. My body protests when I try to bend down to pick them up. Everywhere aches – I wish I could flick a switch and *un*-feel my entire body.

My feet barely fit into my trainers because they are still swollen and sore. The heat affected every part of my body – nowhere escaped.

I walk silently outside into the daylight like a prisoner being guided back to the cells. I look ahead of me and can see nothing but pain. I don't care where I am – to me, this is already a version of hell. I set off limping along the Palm – my body hasn't learnt to be obedient quickly enough yet. It will soon realise that it has no choice in the matter. I decide to run three miles out and three miles back to the resort – six miles or ten kilometres in total. Like a convict hoping for early release. *This is as good as it gets today. Think yourself lucky – it could be worse.* Could it? Really? I'm not so sure.

I begin to cry because I am in so much physical pain. I wish I was anywhere but here. Why am I doing this to myself? Instinctively it feels wrong, but I don't know how to stop. I hobble past some workmen who are covered from head to toe, shielding themselves from the raging heat. I wonder if they can tell how much agony I am in? What would they do if I collapsed, sobbing in the middle of the street? I make a determined effort to fake sanity for the shortest distance until I am past them. Then I am back on my own – just me and my captor – the perfectionist alter ego.

I eventually make it back to the apartment and I collapse on my bed. I don't know it, but this will be a turning point of sorts. Not so long after this, everything will fall apart, and my perfectionist alter ego will be faced with a far greater challenge: *WHAT HAPPENS WHEN I CAN NO LONGER RUN BECAUSE I HAVE COMPLETELY BROKEN MYSELF?* I have written about the impact of that in another book.

When people ask me, 'What happened? Why couldn't you run?', I tell them about a time when running became a dangerous, toxic thing for me because my perfectionist alter ego didn't know when enough was enough. And I can see it so clearly now: on that day, I really, honestly, did enough.

# DAVID

David contacts me after reading a piece in a newspaper in which I'd contributed to an article about running during the Covid pandemic.

*Hi Rachel.*
*I saw your piece in today's* Guardian *and I can massively relate. I have bipolar and running has been keeping me sane during the last year for sure.*
*Let me know if you want to hear more.*
*Cheers.*
*David*

The word 'bipolar' strikes a chord with me straight away, having myself been diagnosed with the condition in my early twenties and prescribed mental health medication for the following decade. So, it is with great interest that I arrange to have a chat with David.

I ask David about his introduction to running and he describes a time during his early to mid-teenage years when running and general fitness was a big part of his life, only to lose it a few years down the line largely thanks to the discovery of beer and girls. It feels like this is a rite of passage into adulthood – to lose those interests that are actually good for us and completely mess things up while on the trepidatious journey through to adulthood. Yup – the box was well and truly ticked for David. Join the club! Our conversation trips along quickly to David's progressive running journey, but I need to press pause. I want to know more about the years before David decided to run a marathon; I want to know how living with bipolar disorder has impacted on his life in the years before and since; and I want to know how running has helped him to manage the condition, especially during the Covid pandemic.

I'm aware that it is quite ridiculous to ask a person when they first began to suffer with bipolar disorder. That's a bit like asking a fish when it first began to swim. Are these things inherent within us, or do they appear out of nowhere – like sprouting a third ear? Nobody can possibly know – and I'd argue that there isn't even a definable 'beginning' to it. That's certainly true for my experience of bipolar disorder. You don't just wake up one morning and it's there – like turning over and seeing a strange face staring at you from the other pillow. Bipolar disorder (like many other mental health struggles) creeps up on you slowly. It is a stealthy illness that doesn't fully reveal itself until there is *absolutely no doubting* that something is very wrong. The frog in a pan analogy is overused, but this illness is exactly that. You don't feel the water temperature rising until it is far too hot.

Anyway, I digress. David explains that he felt the first real signs of his mental illness after his daughter was born, when all the newness and responsibility of parenthood combined with intense pressure at work began to make him notice the creaking of his mental health for the first time. To be honest, it's good to hear a father speak about the newness of parenthood impacting on his mental health. Sure, as women, we have the leading role in parenting – or we certainly do throughout pregnancy as our hormones bend and twist us into the shape of an egg worthy of growing a tiny human being. But let's not forget about the dad's role in all this. David strikes me as somebody who has been deeply impacted by his changing role as father to his little girl. His sense of responsibility sky-rocketed when it became apparent that it wasn't just himself he had to take care of any more; not even just himself and his wife. The introduction of a tiny, helpless human into the mix is a complete rewriting of terms. 'Erm ... excuse me, but was this in the original contract?' ... 'If you look, it was in the small print, Sir.' You see – my years of legal training weren't completely wasted.

The change in David's lifestyle soon impacted on his work. 'Whereas I'd previously stay at work until late into the evening, I now had to tell my colleagues that I *had to* leave at 5 p.m. on the dot, explaining that I needed to pick my daughter up from childcare – while knowing they would often be there until midnight,' David tells me.

Oh, I know the feeling well, as I'm sure many of you do. And of course, this newfound pressure can and does fall on both parents. I remember having to take my daughter, Tilly, to a business meeting when she was just four months old. I ran my own business at the time, and I sat across the desk in a challenging financial meeting with another woman and her male accountant, both wearing smart suits. They shot frequent, pitiful looks across the table as I sat there helplessly nursing my baby as she cried and puked on my top. We were trying to negotiate a business deal. It was awful. I felt like a joker – like somebody who was only half there. Because it's true – only half of me was there! I was busy being a mum while I was also in the middle of a business meeting.

David is explaining something similar, only in a different context. His need to leave work 'early' made him feel as though he was only doing half a job – that is, compared to his career-climbing peers and his pre-fatherhood self. David tells me how he got really, *really* stressed about this (he emphasises the 'really's). 'One day I just started crying,' he says. 'I was crying before work, on the way into work and in the toilets at work. I knew I needed to get some help to avoid things getting really messy.'

Thankfully, David went to see his GP, who signed him off work immediately. During this relatively short period of respite, David recalls experimenting with meditation, which he says helped him to a degree, but he wasn't encouraged to take any physical exercise. This was David's first stark experience of mental illness, but it wouldn't be his last.

A few years later, following a particularly stressful house move, David's mental health illness reared its ugly head again. This time, he was in no doubt what was happening. He knew then that he was suffering with a mental health disorder, and he sought further professional help. 'I just lost the plot,' David tells me, going on to describe how this manifested in his life in various ways, including extravagant and unnecessary spending which resulted in him racking up debt, self-medicating on alcohol and generally living a party lifestyle which he describes as 'completely manic'. Travelling to cities like New York with work didn't help matters, with David indulging in yet more hedonistic behaviour which he was unable to regulate.

Following two serious bouts of acute mental illness and mounting debt, together with an unsustainable lifestyle which was causing havoc with his health, David bravely tells me that he tried to take his own life in 2015. It's shocking to hear anybody say this, but many years ago I realised the tragic reality of suicide when a good friend ended her own life by suicide aged just twenty-six. Like David, she was a 'good laugh'. Just as he is describing his lifestyle, I can picture my effervescent friend on various dancefloors and – like David – she was indeed 'the life and soul of the party'. Suicide doesn't just happen to people who look sad. That outward, bubbly veneer is no indication of what is happening underneath the surface.

After his suicide attempt, David was diagnosed with bipolar disorder. With his family's support and specialist health care, he slowly began making his way back to life. And what I mean by that is the difference between *existing* and *living*. Anyone who has experienced mental health illness will recognise the difference.

One enormous hurdle on David's recovery journey was his return to work. 'It was terrifying,' he tells me. 'In the whole of my life, going back to work following my breakdown was the bravest thing I've ever done.' David explains to me that he was on a managed return-to-work programme, beginning with short hours while he adjusted to his working life again. It was while on his return-to-work plan that David began to connect with nature. 'Initially, I started going out for long walks,' he says. Before long, these walks turned into runs around his local area. 'I began to look forward to going running,' he says. 'It was a highlight in my day.'

David tells me about some challenges that his family faced which added to his levels of stress while he was in recovery, at times threatening to send David's mental health spiralling downwards into further acute episodes. And guess what happened next? The Covid pandemic hit. David was only just treading water with his mental health when the entire world imploded, changing everything we knew overnight. This was perhaps the defining moment for David, when he realised that he needed to take better care of himself. 'I knew I needed to do something to control my frustrations,' he says. David also decided that he wanted to improve his physical health – the motivation coming from his fear of the virus, and it being widely reported that Covid was a greater health risk for those individuals who are obese. The World Obesity Federation states that, 'Obesity-related conditions seem to worsen the effect of Covid-19; indeed, the Centers for Disease Control and Prevention (CDC) reported that people with heart disease and diabetes are at higher risk of Covid-19 complications.'[9]

'I needed to lose a few stone,' David tells me. 'I realised that one thing I could do was to get myself fit and in good shape – and to do that I needed to start running properly.' We've all been there: reaching a point where it's time for us to take back control. This was David's wake-up call. Yes, he'd taken steps to manage his bipolar disorder following some acute episodes of mental illness, but now it was time to take that further, and for him to take a fresh look at his overall health.

Not all of us know what it is like to suffer with bipolar disorder, but all of us *do* know what it is like to manage stresses in our lives, whether they come from the relentlessness of parenthood, pressures at work, family feuds or a global pandemic. It is this part of David's story that strikes me as being particularly poignant, because the truth is that it wasn't until the Covid pandemic hit that he realised the importance of focusing on *all the other aspects of his health* and not just his mental illness. It seems ironic that it took a virus attacking the globe for David to – in his words – 'get his shit together', but I bet he's not alone. I bet many people have had similar epiphanies. For starters, working from home meant that David had more opportunity to get outdoors. 'Running became a thing I would look forward to in my day,' he says. I can relate to this so much. Running with my daughter while home-schooling for nine months was a focus of our daily routine.

It's worth pointing out here that David's running had changed – during the early days of his mental health recovery, he explains that his running was reflective of his mindset. 'Even that was manic,' he tells me. 'I would go too fast on all my runs, and everything felt to be at a crazy pace.

Nothing felt calm.' David paints a vivid picture of somebody who simply didn't know how to find tranquillity and ease with anything in his life, including running. But now, that was about to change. 'I began to slow down and to notice nature,' he says. 'I became more aware of my surroundings and less consumed by my own thoughts.' This is what people describe when they are talking about 'running mindfully' – escaping from your own head and becoming immersed in the beauty around you. That in itself can be a kind of therapy; a pause on the ever-whirring repeat play of 'self'. Finally, thanks to the Covid pandemic, David had started to discover this for himself. He didn't attend any courses; he simply decided to run more slowly and to *be present* instead of chasing – endlessly chasing – something; striving to arrive at a place that never existed. That place was there all along. He just had to slow down to realise it.

David talks to me about the way his bipolar disorder affects him in a cyclical way. 'One of the difficult things for me to manage is this over-whelming surge of energy I get in the springtime,' he tells me. 'It always happens like that and then I slump in winter, like all the energy has drained from my body.'

Bipolar is a mental health disorder steeped in imbalance: chemical imbalances in the brain, and waves of high energy and motivation followed by a terrifying nothingness. This is what David has had to learn to navigate his way around – the ebb and flow of his own mental health illness and working out how best to help himself along the way. When the Covid pandemic hit in the spring of 2020, David was just hitting the peak of his manic tendencies, something he had always struggled to regulate. This used to be the time when he traditionally experienced his most hedonistic, self-destructive behaviour. Once he became aware of the pattern of his illness, it became easier for him to figure out how to avoid falling into that trap. 'I've found that the physical tiredness of running helps me to manage this side of my mental illness,' David says. I've heard other people say the same thing. When you're feeling physically fatigued, it appears as though stressful or invasive thoughts somehow lose their power.

I've never noticed any particularly seasonal patterns to my own mental health issues, but I can certainly relate to the frantic, and at times manic, need to move. Even when you know it's a bad idea; even when your body is screaming 'NO!' I think that talking to David is helping me to realise how this aspect of my personality is a part of my mental health illness, and I have had to learn to deal with it in the same ways that he has done. Could that explain my thought process immediately after the Dubai Marathon? Could it explain my *compulsion* to run – even when any logical, sane person would know that was a bad idea? I think perhaps it can. Could it also help to explain those times when I would struggle to take adequate rest, and the relentless, day-after-day pummelling I put my body through? I can't believe it's taken this conversation with David for me to align my own compulsive behaviour to the very same mental health illness that David and I both share. It is a huge revelation, and it makes me realise all the ways in which I have had to learn to adapt my behaviour – including with the help of CBT therapy – to help me manage my condition. This is a real 'OMG' moment for me.

Running isn't the only discovery in David's post-Covid life. Reflecting on the last eighteen months and the impact of the pandemic, he says, 'It's been a beautiful confluence of things, really. Learning yoga has helped me to slow down and get to know my body, to move more purposefully and understand about mobility.' David tells me that – as a fifteen-stone bloke – stretching is one of his new hobbies. He laughs as he says this, but I think it's fascinating, and I'm really getting a sense of how David's whole mindset has changed. His voice is measured and calm; his sentences are considered. This doesn't sound like a manic person or somebody with the tendency to tear off on a self-destructive bender. How can it even be the same person?

Something else strikes me about David's experience. Running could easily have become a frantic, obsessive focus for his upsurge in energy brought about by his bipolar disorder, but it hasn't become that for him. By combining his other interests of yoga and mindfulness and learning to appreciate being 'in the moment', David has avoided the very trap I fell into. He has managed to keep running safe. I begin to wonder – how did

I get it so wrong?! Whatever the reason, David has managed to find the right balance. And he isn't propagating the idea that running is the *only* answer to his mental health problems. David tells me that he has managed to reduce his mental health medication, but he isn't saying that running is a magic mental health cure. Far from it. In fact, David has now added boxing to the other range of health and wellbeing tools he has discovered to mitigate the impact of bipolar disorder on his life. I guess it's a case of trying different things out and seeing what fits. David has put together a complete self-care package with all the things he needs to remain well, both physically and mentally.

Along the way, David has become very knowledgeable about all things relating to physical fitness, mental health and wellbeing. He speaks eloquently about the well-known benefits of exercise-induced endorphins and the benefits of sleep for mental health – another thing he has found to be vastly improved by running.

David gives full credit to his lovely family for their support along the bumpy road that he has travelled, and to his wife for her ongoing encouragement with his running journey and aspirations, while remaining mindful about the need to remain present and be in the here and now. In balancing out his lifestyle, David is keen to point out that the sociable 'party vibe' is still very much a part of his personality. 'I still enjoy a drink with my wife at the weekend,' he says. 'It's easy to go too far the other way and to lose the things that you need to let your hair down sometimes.' Amen to that! David isn't preaching colonic irrigations and zero carbs. Not at all. He has found a way to balance the opposing sides of his personality, and to remain healthy while allowing himself the freedom to let go now and again. I think it's important to hear this, because many of us do enjoy a beer on a Friday night and not everybody does want to swap that for beetroot juice. David certainly isn't advocating that. He's still up for a pint – just perhaps not ten of them!

Since sharing his story with me, David has completed the 2021 London Marathon in a time of three hours and fifty-six minutes – beating his sub-four-hour marathon goal. 'I started training properly and focused on the

London Marathon at the start of the first lockdown,' David says. He has taken a whopping hour off his marathon time from 2011. As for his goals going forward? 'I need a beer, that's all I know for now!' he says, the day after running the marathon. I can't blame him.

# HELEN

A negative introduction to running is something I can relate to. In the early years when I first put on a pair of running shoes, my own motivation wasn't kick-ass 'This Girl Can' life-affirming mantra. Instead, it was the cruel words and hurtful actions of a toxic ex-boyfriend who made me believe that I was unfit for purpose and that I therefore needed to change myself somehow. By this, I am referring to that non-exhaustive list of dreadful adjectives which can cause the most heartbreaking devastation in a teenage girl, including *thinner, prettier, lighter* and *smaller*. It's an undeniable truth that the running seed isn't always sown in sunny pastures. Sometimes it emerges from a darker place.

Helen struggled with an eating disorder as a teenager. When she didn't *have* to eat, she wouldn't. When she *did* have to eat, she found ways to eliminate the food. One of the many ways of doing this was to run into the woods close to her house and make herself vomit. Admittedly then, Helen didn't have the best introduction to running, using it as a way of 'burning calories' and literally running to a place where she could rid her body of food.

Things got worse for Helen. Following hospitalisation for a burst appendix caused by – amongst other things – eating cotton wool, she confided in her aunt, telling her about her eating disorder. She was immediately referred for some counselling therapy courtesy of the local authority mental health services. One day, during a regular session with her therapist, Helen heard the words she dreaded the most: 'Well, it looks as though we're not getting anywhere here, so it might be time to involve your parents.'

This prospect shocked Helen to her core. To put this into some context, 'Helen' isn't her real name. The reason for this is that even all these years later, she doesn't want her parents to find out the full extent of her mental health maelstrom during her younger years. 'They have a "get a bloody grip" attitude towards mental health,' she tells me. Helen was so terrified of the response from her parents that she reluctantly began to take steps towards tackling some of her disordered eating behaviours, and her therapy started to turn a corner and became more effective as a result. She noticed that due to her body finally receiving some of the nutrition it so desperately needed, her running began to improve. From this point in Helen's life, she began to turn to running as a way of managing stress in her life.

Helen tells me a little about her early childhood. When she was as young as six or seven years old, she was already aware of certain foods being labelled 'good' or 'bad' and, although she doesn't wish to apportion any blame on specific individuals for this, she explains that this is where she believes her obsession with food came from. 'My mum was always on a diet and my stepmum was permanently aware of not only what *she* was eating, but what the rest of us were eating, too. As a child it was something I picked up on and I became hyper-aware of food, as though it was something I should be constantly vigilant about.'

I think back to my own mum's disordered eating and all the tiny ways it manifested in our everyday lives. The enormous meals she would prepare and never eat herself; the 'too busy to eat' excuses and the non-meals made up of digestive biscuits and cups of tea. The avoidance and diversion tactics: she made sure that we were all too busy eating and becoming satiated, which took any attention away from the fact that she was visibly shrinking. I see it all so clearly now, just as Helen does with her own experience of the same.

Helen had a different body shape to her younger sister, who she describes as being 'built like a grasshopper'. To even be aware of a purportedly 'more desirable' female body shape and size at such a young age is repugnant, but as a woman who has also experienced the judgement of others – including close family members – based on that factor alone, I can completely see how this sent Helen's young mind into a head spin of anxiety and confusion about food, eating and her changing body. All the clues are there. *Of course* she would go on to develop an eating disorder! *Of course* she would grow up to be fearful over calories and see certain foods as 'good' or – mostly – 'bad'. *Of course* she would grow up to loathe her changing adolescent body and try to keep herself in a certain 'acceptable' shape and size to please those judgemental adults around her. *Of course* she would find ways to rid her body of the energy she was forced to ingest, out of sight, in the woods and completely alone.

Fortunately, we can share a laugh about our bond over these shared aspects of our childhoods, but I still feel a deep sadness listening to Helen and imagining a little girl torn to pieces by a world she simply didn't understand.

Once again, we hit a bingo in the other labels we were given as young adolescents. 'My brother was good at building things, whereas I was the academic one,' she says. But Helen didn't *feel* like she was academic or that she could fulfil that role, and she didn't particularly want to. Worse still, the pedestal on which she was placed was raised ever higher. *This girl does well at school ... This girl gets good exam results ... This girl doesn't get into trouble ... This girl comes home on time ... This girl is the 'golden child'.* Helen was given no room to make mistakes, to learn and grow. She was given no room to breathe.

In addition to Helen being placed on the 'good girl' pedestal, she struggled to work out where she belonged in a family which struggled with dysfunctionality, including strained step-parent dynamics and some domestic abuse. 'I was constantly in this battle,' she tells me. 'I would go to my dad's and I'd be asked why I'm not at my mum's; I'd go to my mum's and I'd witness the abuse.' How could she possibly know where to fit in or to feel safe, being bounced between one struggling parent and the other in varying degrees of chaos and confusion? There was precious little consistency for Helen to anchor herself to. One parent would allow her to go and play outside, while the other one wouldn't – for no apparent reason. She would often busy herself doing homework on the computer, living up to the 'good girl' image, and that would be okay sometimes – but then she would randomly be shouted at and told to 'get off it' and 'go and write it out on paper' instead. No reason was given. 'In a world where I had absolutely no control over anything at all, I was desperate to have control over something,' she says. That is perfectly understandable, and it is where her obsession with food and running originates.

I have a vivid picture in my mind of Helen as a child: confused, unsettled, an over-thinker, a high-achiever. A young girl who turns in on herself in response to the emotional shrapnel she is being bombarded with on a daily basis. She is surrounded by many broken adults who are struggling themselves to survive. My own view is that as parents, we try our best given the experiences we have endured in life, but there is a tiny part of us all which remains broken – even in a small way – and as hard as we might try, we can't help but pass on some of that debris to our children. I think of it as damage limitation. Even the best parents (decided on an entirely arbitrary rationale) manage to get it wrong and mess it up sometimes. We all do it – despite our best efforts. Nobody is perfect. This being the case, I can totally see Helen's deep-rooted need to control *something* in her life.

By taking steps towards managing her disordered eating – the *one thing in the world* she had any control over – Helen paradoxically felt like she was surrendering in some way. She had given up the tiny element of power she had over her own life. It was a sacrifice and a real sense of loss to her, and so she needed to find something to replace it.

Helen moved away to university, where her running continued. Her recollections include observing that everyone at university seemed to be 'bigger and scarier and more grown-up' than she was. She felt like a tiny person who was pretending to be an adult but who was still very much a child in her own head, without any idea how to make sense of the grown-up world around her. I knew that Helen and I would bond! Right from her first messages to me, it felt like we had many things in common. We make a deal: 'When I find out what the hell we're supposed to do as adults,' Helen says, 'I promise I will let you know.' I'm holding her to that.

At university, certain aspects of student life worked well for Helen, while others felt completely alien. 'I quite enjoyed going out for an occasional drink with my uni mates, but I hated going clubbing. It was far too loud and I didn't like getting drunk and staying out until four in the morning,' she says.

While her university friends were busy nursing hangovers, Helen occupied herself by pursuing her interests of running and long-distance walking. Gradually, the two began to morph into one another. Enter stage left her new love: long-distance running. 'For the first time in my life, people began to notice me in a positive way and say, "Bloody hell, Helen – you're actually quite good at this!"' she tells me.

This was a pivotal point for Helen – one where for the first time in her life she felt visible, and she was acknowledged as being 'good' at something that she actually enjoyed. *Bingo!* The feeling is so familiar to me, and I can tell you that it feels rather like discovering a life-enhancing drug. For both Helen and me, this was the moment when our self-worth became inextricably fused with our sense of newfound visibility and accomplishment, and our egos would become hooked on the feeling. We would both try harder and harder and push ourselves beyond what is reasonable to ask – or demand – of our bodies. We are now running addicts, our self-worth only sustained by the running equivalent of crack cocaine, without any idea how difficult it will be to withdraw.

As with any other hard drug, initially there is a high. 'I started running more and more and it felt great!' Helen tells me … but I already know where this story is heading. This is all too painfully familiar. Of course, it feels fantastic to get recognition for being good at something following a childhood of low self-esteem and purported mediocrity – or worse. And while this is a book about the many positive aspects of running and the myriad ways in which people have been helped and even saved by it, this is a reality check. When self-worth attaches itself to running and performance – even for non-professional, everyday runners like myself and Helen – it can be a very dangerous thing.

Helen began entering races and was soon taking part in half-marathon events pretty much every weekend. I know only too well how addictive it can be. I remember running – and winning – a twenty-mile road race one Saturday in autumn 2016 and forcing myself to race in the Great North Run the following weekend, knowing full well that my legs hadn't recovered. It is this compulsion that Helen was also experiencing, as though there simply wasn't the option to step off the bus and rest for a little while.

As though if we did stop, then we would return immediately to the land of mediocrity whence we came – rather like landing on a snake in a game of snakes and ladders and slip-sliding our way right back down to the bottom. The only way we could contemplate moving forward is to push ourselves harder – that is the way our brains are wired. We don't know any different.

Helen suffered from mild hypothermia during a particularly brutal storm while running her first marathon. What is even worse is that because of the severity of Helen's condition, which required her to be taken by ambulance to hospital at mile twenty of the race, she saw her eating disorder re-emerge with a vengeance. Following that dreadful marathon, Helen's unruly mind went into overdrive. Her boyfriend ordered a takeaway and expected Helen to tuck into the mountain of Indian food generously spread across the kitchen table, but she was only able to pick at tiny morsels, her head screaming at her: *'You didn't even finish the marathon! You don't need to eat this food! DO NOT EAT IT!'* Helen had run twenty miles of the marathon; she had been treated in hospital for mild hypothermia. And yet, her mind was unable to wrangle her out of the *'YOU DID NOT COMPLETE THIS MARATHON ... YOU MUST NOT EAT!'* debilitating headlock. Just like my head would not allow me to be okay with my 'poor performance' at the Dubai Marathon and I suffered so badly as a result, so Helen's mind would not allow her to get off scot-free. There was a price to be paid for her apparent 'failure', and Helen was once again submerged in the eating disorder which she had up to that point managed to curtail.

The shocking way in which both of us have experienced a resurgence of a mental health illness following our inability to process the less-than-desirable outcome of a marathon is glaring.

After that awful marathon experience, Helen's mental wellbeing hit the floor. She felt lost, her head swimming with a sense of 'Okay – what do I do now?', which perhaps hit her so much harder than it might have done because of the fleeting glimpse of recognition and validation she had experienced since her progression and achievement through running. It is a difficult balance to strike and a very narrow ledge on which the ego and self-worth must perch. 'I asked myself, "Where do I go from here?"' she says. 'I used to spend most of my annual leave going on long training runs, and without that as a focus, I honestly didn't know what to do. I struggled to cope.'

When Helen says that she 'struggled', what she actually means is that mentally, she was at breaking point. Her whole focus and drive, and all her time and energy that had gone into running, was now displaced. It had nowhere to go. And so, she turned to drink. 'I would just get shit-faced,' she says. And as desperate as it sounds, it is also perfectly understandable.

To get over the horror of her first marathon, Helen set her sights on another marathon and pushed herself more than she had ever done before. Interestingly, she still refers to herself as having 'failed' at her first marathon, despite the adverse conditions and suffering hypothermia which was so severe that she required hospital treatment.

I know the pattern.

Helen's diary was soon crammed with races – her calendar was jam-packed and her training schedule was relentless. She completed her next marathon, but *still* her mind wouldn't allow her to celebrate any moment of victory. Finishing that marathon in a respectable time of four hours and ten minutes, Helen immediately began chastising herself for not running faster, especially since she had found the race to be perfectly manageable. Flashbacks of the Dubai Marathon and all the ensuing devastation floods my mind. How could we be so hard on ourselves? How did running become *yet another thing* for us to beat ourselves up over? Why were our best efforts – despite horrific conditions – simply not good enough? Would they *ever* be enough? It's taken me a long time to understand that the way my mind worked on that day was incredibly damaging to me – both physically and even more so mentally. I wonder if Helen has had the same realisation.

Sadly, Helen fell back into the old trap of racing more and more on an endless quest for improvement. My heart sinks as she tells me this. It feels like watching someone self-harming, but in a sense that's what this is. Unable to accept ourselves or believe that we are 'good enough', we push harder – until we break.

For a while, Helen's half-marathon time improved week-on-week. People in her running club watched in amazement as she was slicing chunks off her personal best times. But the truth lingering behind this purported progress was a grim and devastating one of a person desperately trying to prove her own worth – with no apparent destination in mind and no way of knowing if or when she would ever get there. And it's worth mentioning here the juxtaposition between the external validation and the inner turmoil. Every time Helen received some acknowledgement or recognition for her success and improvement, ironically that fed into her chimp's mantra to *'try harder'* and *'do more'*. I know as well as anyone how utterly soul-destroying this feels, as it is ultimately being motivated by fear for continued success and improvement. And that well will dry out pretty damn quickly.

Of course, this would all come crashing down. Following an MRI scan, Helen discovered a stress fracture in her hip and a whole ream of other health struggles. Endless tales of hospital appointments, scans, GP and consultant visits later, and she was unable to run at all – barely even able to walk at times. Helen was understandably devastated. 'The *one thing* I could control; the *one thing* that I was actually pretty good at, all of a sudden I couldn't do.' I feel her sense of loss. It is palpable. But this is what happens when our self-worth and sense of wellbeing becomes so entangled with running that there is nothing else to fall back on.

Helen was referred for counselling therapy to help her to manage the many demons she was battling, and even some of the people closest to her weren't aware of the depths of her pain or feelings of loss. 'They would say, "It's only running!"' Helen tells me, and we both laugh out loud. Not because that is funny in any sense, but because it is so ludicrous in the context of the role that running has played in our mental health. To minimise the impact of a loss like this is even worse for a person like myself or Helen, diminishing our mental health struggles as though they are futile or self-indulgent; or as though we have any choice in the matter.

Thankfully, I've had the time to reflect on my own experiences and to seek out the help that I needed to pull me from that place. I've since learnt many survival strategies and I've tackled some of the underlying demons which I believe were a root cause of my running addiction, but sadly, Helen is not as far along her journey. At the time of writing, she is still awaiting a hip operation and she is still determined to return to running just as soon as her body will allow. I can only hope that Helen somehow manages to extrapolate running from her self-esteem, and that she can discover running again in a healthier context – one where a certain race outcome is not indicative of her self-worth.

Since sharing her story with me, Helen has completed a trail race just four days before surgery on her hip. 'It was really special having one last race before being out for months,' she tells me. Going forward, her goals are to recover from her operation and then combine her love of travel and marathon running. 'I'd like to complete as many international marathons as possible,' she says. I sincerely hope that Helen takes care of herself – both physically and mentally – on her recovery journey.

# KATHRYN

I remember it so well myself – the time when buying bottles of wine was no longer sufficient, so I began buying *boxes* of the stuff instead. Imagine that – getting to a point in your life where the prospect of arriving home from a hard day at work to open the fridge door and find only enough for one small glass left in the bottle was a prospect so truly hideous that – just to avoid that happening – I made sure I had *two litres* of it chilling in a box, instead. It remains etched in my mind – the progression from bottles to boxes of wine – as being symbolic of a time in my life when I self-medicated on alcohol and Prozac. And it isn't like that was for just a short period of time, either. This happened for *years*. Plus – even more shocking – I was, on the surface at least, entirely functional throughout this time. I qualified as a solicitor; I held down a job; I bought my own home and fed and watered my four rescue cats. It was like drowning in full view.

Kathryn has spent most of her adult life being alcohol dependent. And she doesn't mean in the damaging-yet-manageable context of having boxes instead of bottles of wine. She means in the deepest, gut-wrenching, organ-failing sense of the word.

Kathryn was an alcoholic. And it almost killed her.

'I began drinking when I was fourteen, and now I've had the chance to reflect back on my relationship with alcohol, I understand that I drank to change the way I felt,' she says. It is only early in our conversation, but already Kathryn is one of the most honest and articulate people I have ever met. She has written blogs about her journey with alcoholism and has opened herself up in a way that few people are able to do. 'I've moved past my own shame,' she tells me. 'I've had to do that in order to move forward with my life.'

Not only did alcohol seem to be effective in changing Kathryn's emotional state throughout her teenage years, but when she went to college as a young person, she genuinely believed that drinking gave her confidence, enhanced her character and made her 'fun' to be around. I'm sure many of us can relate to this – the lie that alcohol improves everything (including ourselves), when in fact it creates a cycle of misery and dependency and blocks the very feelings that need addressing in the first place. Kathryn was in a long-term self-medicating relationship with alcohol, and she firmly believed that she couldn't function without it.

It's important to mention that Kathryn was in an emotionally abusive relationship at the time – one where there were no visible scars for anybody to see, but the emotional damage to her and her children was massive. 'My children were living in a highly toxic environment,' she tells me. 'And rather than get us out of it, I tried to hide from it in booze.'

Kathryn doesn't try to mask the fact that her children suffered as a direct result of her drinking, but she has the bravery to stand up and accept that her role as a mother was seriously compromised because of it. Lamenting regret and shame isn't Kathryn's style. She has long since come to terms with the reality of her children's experience growing up, and I am amazed by the way she holds herself fully accountable while not allowing herself to be submerged in a sea of deep shame. I believe the Oprah-inspired phrase is 'taking ownership' for her part, and I so admire Kathryn's strength of character for being able to hold herself fully accountable while letting go of the self-hatred. That must be a difficult thing to do.

By the end of Kathryn's addiction to alcohol, she was drinking around the clock. 'I actually hoped that I would drink myself to death, because I was too pathetic to even take my own life.' Kathryn describes her entire life as being centred around getting hold of alcohol, drinking it and disposing of the empties, while trying to maintain an image to the outside world of a person who was functioning in society. Can you imagine that?

Kathryn lost almost everything as a result of her alcohol dependency. 'I have three children, and my two eldest walked out as soon as they could,' she tells me. 'It was a long time coming, but eventually I was dragged along to an alcohol-dependency service by my brother. He told me that if I didn't sort myself out, he would involve the social services over the care of my youngest child.' Kathryn now works in drug and alcohol services, and she considers it a small miracle that she avoided intervention and possibly the removal of her youngest child. 'Nowadays, that would have happened without a doubt,' she tells me.

Kathryn was in poor physical health, her blood pressure was sky high and she was seriously overweight. At this crossroads in her life, she was faced with a stark choice. She decided that she needed to focus on something other than the loss and restriction of simply 'not drinking'. I guess it's rather like the self-help books which advise against setting yourself negative goals. Instinctively, Kathryn knew what she must do. 'I couldn't have succeeded if I'd only focused on the alcohol – or the abstinence from it,' she says. That makes perfect sense to me. Kathryn needed to focus her mind on something positive, far away from any thoughts about alcohol which – admittedly – she didn't even want to give up in the first place. 'I decided to create an entire wellbeing package,' Kathryn tells me. 'I wanted to focus on all the other aspects of my health rather than on abstinence or losing weight, which seemed to be so negative and reminded me of all that I would be losing, instead of all that I would gain from learning how to look after my body and my mind in a healthy way.'

It is the best decision she ever made.

Kathryn's inner resilience began to emerge when instead of going on prescribed medication for certain health conditions, she asked her GP to give her three months to turn her life around. This is the first glimmer of Kathryn demonstrating her desire to regain control over her own health and to take whatever steps she could to wrestle back her quality of life. She would require a complete overhaul of her general wellbeing, including a basic fitness plan and learning all she could about healthy nutrition.

Kathryn is a very matter-of-fact, practical person. Once the decision was made, she immediately went online and ordered herself a pair of cheap trainers and some basic training kit, and she downloaded the Couch to 5k app which had been recommended to her by a friend. Kathryn also took advantage of her local council's fitness incentive whereby she could use the local gym a few times a week for free. No stone was left unturned in her efforts to redesign her life and use every means available to her. Kathryn found the resources and the help she needed. She didn't have lots of money to throw at this, but what she did have was determination in bucketloads.

'Initially I was too embarrassed to run outside,' she tells me, 'so the option to use the local gym was brilliant for me.' Kathryn took herself off to the local leisure centre and typically chose the treadmill which was hidden out of sight in a dimly lit corner of the fitness room. And so began the very first tentative steps towards her new life.

This part of Kathryn's journey resonates strongly with me. The memory of taking those very first wobbly steps forward when the biggest battle is the fear of looking foolish. I believe that this is where true bravery is born; in not letting the nasty chimp convince you to not even bother trying because *you're making a fool of yourself*. Bravery is walking into the gym with a baggy T-shirt on and stepping on the treadmill in the corner *despite* those cruel taunts. It is turning up regardless, even when you don't feel like you belong in a gym or that your body can run on a treadmill. It is making all the tiny choices to keep going and the daily refusal to give in to that voice – the one that is telling you to stop.

Kathryn explains that much of the physical damage caused by alcohol – organ failure, brain damage, liver fibrosis, stroke and cardiomyopathy amongst others – doesn't become evident until it's too late. Thankfully, the damage to Kathryn's body was not irreversible. Yes, she had caused some health issues, but thankfully she had not crossed the threshold from which there is no return. 'When I found out that I wasn't physically damaged beyond repair, I felt an immediate sense of determination, like I owe it to my body to take better care of it. I was so relieved – I felt like I'd dodged a bullet,' she tells me. Having expected the worst, Kathryn felt she had been given a second chance at life.

And so, following the Couch to 5k training plan, the complete overhaul of Kathryn's health and wellbeing continued … and it built momentum. Nutrition, structured training, meditation, mental wellbeing: it was all up for grabs. The Couch to 5k app was hugely motivational for Kathryn.

'I religiously ticked off my three sessions a week and I did exactly what the lady [on the app] told me to do. It gave me a focus and a structure, and both of those things were vital for me and my recovery,' she says.

This is where Kathryn the hero was born.

Kathryn started to feel much better, and she began to lose some weight. After successfully completing the Couch to 5k programme, she decided that she would try running outside for the very first time: another step forward in being brave. While out on one of her very first runs along the unfamiliar canal, she decided that she wanted to take part in the London Marathon. 'It makes me laugh now, because I'd only ever run eight kilometres up to that point, but it was right at the time when the ballot places were open for the London Marathon, and I decided that I wanted to run it for Guide Dogs for the Blind.'

Kathryn's goal to run the London Marathon so early in her running journey may seem lofty to some, but she's in good company. I totally understand her commitment to that journey. Kathryn tells me that her mum was blind and she had guide dogs all her life, which is why she felt compelled to run for the Guide Dogs charity. 'It felt like the universe helped to make it happen,' she says, on receiving the news that she had indeed secured a charity place. Kathryn soon discovered that running became her therapy. As she built up the miles in preparation for the 2017 London Marathon, a realisation dawned on her that running was fundamental for her mental health. She made it to the start and across the finish line of that marathon and raised money for the Guide Dogs charity which was so close to her heart. 'My mum and auntie were supporting me on the day,' she says, describing how they were excitedly tracking her on the app. 'They were so proud.'

Kathryn says that she feels lucky because she can now talk about her alcoholism with all three of her children, while many others don't get the chance – the children often walking away from the alcohol-dependent parent as soon as they are able to do so, thereby leading to the complete disintegration of the family with no recourse to repair the damage caused by the addiction. The honesty with which Kathryn holds up her hands and doesn't try to diminish the devastating impact of her alcoholism on her children is brave and astounding. 'I may be fully recovered and healthy now I'm five years sober – and I may be living the best life I possibly can, but my children are growing into adulthood still carrying the scars of their childhood with an alcoholic parent. They will need to find their own pathway to deal with that. The normalisation of alcohol and its everyday use means that there's a lot of misunderstanding about its effect and the destruction it can have on a family,' she says.

We all know that alcohol changes a person. You can feel different after just a few drinks. 'My children grew up not knowing from one moment to the next which version of their mum they would be faced with,' Kathryn says. 'There is little understood about the long-term impact of that on a child. The emotional unavailability of the parent means that the children of alcoholics can grow up with attachment issues. That just isn't talked about.'

I tell Kathryn about the time I spent working at a local alcohol and drug dependency service during the years when my work involved supporting local charitable organisations. I rocked up there a few times a week and served full English breakfasts to those who relied on the weekly free cooked meals; I washed the greasy pots in a stainless steel sink the size of a small bathtub; but most of all, I talked to people who were in the process of their own recovery. I was not only fascinated by the individual stories of how life had led them to alcohol addiction and then to the place that would potentially save them, but I was amazed by the fact that these were not the 'down and outs' that I'd been led to believe experienced drug and alcohol dependency. They were talented artists and poets, writers and craftsmen. I met a guy called Andy who played the piano like I've never heard it played before. I read poems written by a man called Paul which brought me to tears. I was simply astounded that these were the type of people accessing this service. They weren't 'layabouts' or 'good-for-nothings'. They were ordinary people just like you and me, and Kathryn. Speaking to Kathryn once again reminds me that alcoholism and addiction isn't based on class or wealth or education or any of those superfluous things. It can and does wreck the lives of people across the board. Or – in Kathryn's case – it comes perilously close.

Kathryn's strength was put to the test in early 2018 when her mum died

– a time of great trauma when some of the people closest to Kathryn feared that this would prompt her to start drinking again. 'As horrendously difficult as that time was, and as fully committed as I was to abstain from drinking alcohol, I knew that I needed running to keep me on track,' she says. This is surely a true test if ever there was one. And remember that this was less than two years since Kathryn had begun on her recovery journey – it was still very early days. I ask her why she believes this wasn't a catalyst for her to relapse, and she simply says, 'By that time, I had developed a full and comprehensive self-care package, so I firmly believe that my all-encompassing approach to my physical and mental wellbeing helped me to avoid the pitfall that experiencing the loss of my mum could otherwise have been.'

I think this speaks volumes for the way in which Kathryn chose to redesign her life completely and not just focus on one linear aspect of her recovery – including the refusal to limit herself to a negative, restrictive approach by simply 'not drinking'. This enabled her to take full advantage of the many other benefits of a comprehensively healthy lifestyle – including different coping mechanisms for her mental health. She says, 'I knew the things I needed to do to stay well.' This has such a profound effect on me. For Kathryn to have come back from the brink of a life completely in tatters courtesy of decades of alcohol addiction to a place where she had designed her own self-care package which was powerful enough to keep her safe *despite* the loss of her mum – I am simply in awe. This is the very essence of a person taking their life by the reins and making a deliberate choice to steer it in a completely different direction. This is about a person taking full accountability for their decisions and taking back control. This is a person realising that their life has value, that *they* have value. This is about self-worth. Kathryn had her anchors firmly in place when she could so easily have nose-dived into a relapse. And she has relied on her self-care package ever since. 'I had my heart badly broken at the beginning of 2020,' she tells me. 'But again, I had my anchors to keep me safe. I knew how to survive and how to be okay. Keeping myself physically well has helped me to stay in a good place mentally, so I know that the two are interlinked.'

It is entirely unrealistic to think that once you set off on a path of recovery from any place – including alcohol dependency – that progress will continue to follow an upward trajectory and there will be no further bumps in the road. That just isn't life. Progress isn't linear. If only it were that simple. Kathryn's story demonstrates true resilience because she was able to weather the storms when they arrived – when her mum died, when she was left heartbroken by a failed relationship, and by the devastating impact of the Covid-19 pandemic. Any of these life events could have thrown Kathryn completely off track and back into her old behaviours, but they didn't.

'One of the familiar patterns I've seen as a practitioner [in alcohol recovery services] is a belief that if a person stops drinking, then all their problems will go away, and that simply isn't the case,' Kathryn says. 'The problems don't go away. Life is still there. The important thing is to build healthier coping mechanisms for when things do happen – which they will – to knock you off track.' This sounds like such an obvious thing when Kathryn says it, but I can totally imagine a person becoming so focused on liberation from alcohol dependency that they forget to consider the 'what-ifs' and plan for the curveballs that life will throw at them. Kathryn believes that this is why it is important to put positive, purposeful goals in place to strengthen resolve for such times, and to remember that abstinence alone is not a silver bullet for all of life's problems; it is simply one major step forward in being able to deal with them effectively.

Kathryn talks to me about learning to 'sit with the pain' rather than to feel compelled to drink and escape from it, whatever that pain is – bereavement, the breakdown of a relationship, abuse. Learning how to be still and allow herself to be with the pain rather than do anything – including drinking herself into oblivion – to try and run away from it was a fundamental part of Kathryn's recovery.

Kathryn identified one aspect of her newfound self-care toolkit – specifically running – as potentially lending itself to certain behaviour patterns. Although not keen to label herself as having a specific 'personality type', she recognised her tendency towards obsessive behaviours, and so to avoid allowing this to push her into overtraining, she enlisted the help of a running coach. From my own experiences and tendency towards overtraining, I think the insight that Kathryn had into her own vulnerabilities and the need to protect herself from this aspect of her personality is incredibly astute. 'I realised very early on that I could end up breaking myself,' she says. To have such self-awareness at any time, let alone in the early days of recovery, is simply astounding. 'With the grief of losing my mum, there were times when I could easily have gone out for a hard run and still been running five hours later, so I had to manage that and get it under control.'

I can strongly relate to this side of Kathryn's personality and her inclination towards not knowing when to stop – especially in times of inner turmoil. I remember going out for a 'short' run when Tilly was just a tiny baby and coming back fourteen miles later, almost inducing a search party rescue incident; I recall running in the snow when my relationship was in turmoil and returning home so cold and hypothermic that I passed out on the bathroom floor. It is like having zero ability to rationalise and to moderate yourself – as though that channel has been switched off in my brain. The adage 'You don't know when to stop!' is surely derived from actions of a person like myself or Kathryn. They're right – we don't know when to stop! Everybody is different, and we all have our challenges, but neither I nor Kathryn need any help with motivation to get us out the front door. Both of us *do* need help with knowing when to hold back, when to ease off and when to stop. Just as we once gravitated towards other behaviours to numb ourselves emotionally, so we can do the same with running and gorge ourselves on it until we are sick – the running equivalent of Bruce Bogtrotter and the chocolate cake.

Kathryn still has the same running coach four years on, and she explains that this not only makes her accountable, but it ensures that she doesn't damage herself in pursuing her running and triathlon goals, which have progressed rather significantly since the Couch to 5k programme. 'Running was such a big part of my self-care package that I couldn't risk losing it to the obsessive part of my personality which could so easily have turned running into a thing I would use to break myself.'

I wish I'd had Kathryn's level of self-awareness back in the days when my ego allowed running to eat me up and spit me out. I need to remind myself that Kathryn was in recovery from a lifetime of severe alcohol dependency at the time *and* dealing with the grief of losing her mother, and she was *still* able to put these safety mechanisms in place to maintain her self-care package. Kathryn wasn't out to find a 'quick fix' for her struggles. She was fully committed to discovering a long-term, sustainable strategy that would keep her safe, regardless of life's rollercoaster twists and turns. I find it completely staggering.

And that's without even considering the pressures of social media. 2016 was a big year for social media 'influencers'. 'It was very difficult for me not to get sucked into the whole vibe of who could run the most miles in a month, endless "runstreaks" and other "DO MORE!" messages which could have potentially been very damaging for me,' Kathryn says.

She firmly believes that having a run coach enabled her to stay safe when it would have been so easy to get washed away in the social media hype. It's a timely reminder of the power of the messages we see online every single day. Have you ever scrolled through Instagram and every other person seems to have completed a 100k ultra run at the weekend? Have you looked on Strava and seen that somebody in your local area has run a hilly twenty-miler with 3,000-foot elevation before breakfast that morning while you struggled to complete a local 10k loop? For people like myself and Kathryn, seeing posts like this can be inspiring, but they can also be a dangerous lure into the 'DO MORE! WORK HARDER!' slippery slope which ended up in my dreadful experience the day after the Dubai Marathon in that very year – 2016. Especially for those of us with personality types which lend themselves to obsessive behaviour patterns and addictive traits, it can be a red flag – a warning to BEWARE! One addiction can just as easily be replaced with another; it's about learning how to moderate our thinking and our behaviour patterns and to consider them in a more holistic way, as Kathryn had the foresight to do. In my view, that is true recovery. It is genuine strength – the strength not to get sucked into *another* unhealthy compulsive behaviour because we haven't learnt how to sit with our own pain. This is the part of Kathryn's story I find so compelling and so inspiring: having the strength not only to begin to run from a place of zero fitness

– and, worse, a body damaged following years of abuse – but the resilience to create a long-term strategy and to commit to that when it would be so easy to be blindsided by everything from grief to a broken heart and even succumbing to social media pressures.

Kathryn has seen the benefits of staying away from social media hype, and by sticking to her coach's plan, she has seen vast improvements in her performance. 'You don't improve by constantly chasing segments on Strava,' she says, smiling (we've all been there). 'You improve by following a plan. I know that my coach has got my back, and I've learnt to trust the process.' She says this with such confidence and self-assurance – it feels like it is Kathryn's journey which began over a decade ago, and not mine. I've had to learn this the hard way, but it is delightful to hear that Kathryn has the support mechanisms in place to ensure that running remains a pivotal part of her self-care package for a long time to come.

Kathryn's first London Marathon was – in her words – 'transformational'. 'If I could go from Couch to 5k to running a marathon in the space of a year, I truly believed that anything was possible.' The transformational power of running a marathon is something I can truly relate to. Kathryn and I can look back and consider the places we have come from, knowing that we have overcome our personal challenges – mine was mental health illness; Kathryn's was alcoholism. When we fully absorb that journey and all the tiny, sometimes huge, and often painful steps it has taken to get us there, we both experienced a sense of unlocking a door of possibility for the very first time – allowing ourselves to peek through and see a sign saying 'dare to dream'. I know that happened to me back in 2011, and it's clear that Kathryn experienced the same thing in 2017. 'When I finished the marathon, I had a strong sense that I can do anything! And not just in terms of physical fitness, but in other areas of my life,' she says. I think this is a crucial point: the door of possibility isn't just unlocked on a person's fitness potential, but on all other aspects of their life. The knock-on effects can be far-reaching and include all sorts of life-changing decisions.

Kathryn's newfound confidence following her first London Marathon was a catalyst for her to change direction and pursue a career in alcohol recovery services. 'I'd always abandoned myself completely,' she says.

'I'd never focused on anything I wanted to achieve professionally before, but this time, something had changed.'

We know what had changed. Kathryn had finally discovered her self-belief and she had started to prioritise *her* goals for once. She undertook various qualifications and followed the steps required – rather like a marathon training plan – and is now a manager in a substance abuse recovery service.

After the London Marathon, Kathryn decided to pursue two major fitness goals. Firstly, she has set her sights on qualifying with a Good for Age place for the London Marathon; and secondly, she decided to pursue her interest in triathlon. 'I wanted to take my running towards a sub-four-hour marathon whilst at the same time learning how to ride a road bike [from zero experience] and learning how to swim front crawl [she could only swim breaststroke].'

I know how challenging and time-consuming it is to focus on improving your marathon running to the point of obtaining a GFA place, but to combine this with triathlon training is quite an undertaking. Once again, Kathryn astounds me with her goals, which may seem daunting to some, but are surely nowhere near as frightening as the life she could have been living had she not made that decision to get clean.

I am in awe of Kathryn's journey and the message of hope it sends to other people who may be suffering with addiction of any kind and struggling to find a way out. I am astounded by her levels of self-awareness and her honesty, her ability to face up to the truth of the addiction she has overcome and her refusal to live in shame. I am in awe of her personal courage and her desire to help others, not only in her professional work but by setting an example of just what can be achieved with the right levels of commitment, determination and belief. And it comes down to that word – belief. Running a marathon enabled Kathryn to believe that she could be free from alcohol addiction, and she could completely redesign her life. And that is certainly something worth celebrating.

Since sharing her story with me, Kathryn went on to complete her second full Ironman event in August 2021. When I ask her about her proudest running moment, she tells me that this was running the Manchester

Marathon in 2018 shortly after her mum had died, and just three days after her mum's funeral. 'It was touch and go whether I would even make it to the start line,' she says. 'Running that marathon was the race I finished for her.'

Following her recent Ironman event, Kathryn is taking some time off to recover, but she will soon be in training for her goal of achieving a sub-four-hour marathon in Manchester in the spring.

# RACHAEL

I always love meeting other Rachels, especially ones who have discovered the joys of running. It doesn't matter that we are separated by a single vowel in the spelling of our name: when Rachael (with an a) contacts me to share her story, I am simply delighted. Her message to me reads:

> *Hi Rachel.*
> *Up until 2015 I'd barely run anywhere – except for last orders at the bar!*
> *I was unhealthy, I smoked and drank, and – up to 2011 – I was a single*
> *parent who struggled with depression and loneliness. I'd been on and off*
> *antidepressants for years …*

This story rings many bells with me already, but she's barely even started. Rachael's story is about the healing and transformative power of running not just for herself, but for her husband, following the devastating loss of their baby in 2013. The couple will go on a journey together through the darkest moments imaginable and they will come back stronger, healthier and more resilient than they had ever thought possible. Rachael's story is about the strength of running to transform *both* their lives, and to open their worlds to the restorative power of a loving and supportive running community. In short, the couple will be completely transformed by running, and they will never look back.

Like so many of us, Rachael had felt distanced from sport and running throughout her teens. 'I used to like running when I was younger, but then in my teenage years I lost it completely. I guess I discovered more exciting things to do,' she says. Those 'more exciting things' were the usual adolescent trappings of socialising with friends, drinking Hooch and dating. Why is it necessary for most of us to wade through this period of purported enlightenment only to discover years down the line how unhealthy and futile it all is? That's a question for another day. For now, though, Rachael will wave goodbye to her physical fitness and she won't revisit it until she is years down the line in her late twenties.

Rachael met her husband, Billy, in 2011 and she tells me that their 'unhealthy lifestyle' (her words) continued in tandem. In 2013 the couple were delighted to discover that Rachael was pregnant with their first child. Rachael recalls talking to a midwife at one of her prenatal appointments who was running in the Great North Run – the world-famous half marathon that takes place in Rachael's home city of Newcastle. 'I remember saying to Billy, "I'm going to run that one day",' she says, admitting that at the time, she was barely fit enough to walk up a flight of stairs, let alone run a half marathon. Billy was understandably sceptical, but although neither of them realised it at the time, a tiny seed had just been sown in Rachael's mind. Neither Rachael nor Billy thought any more about it as Rachael's pregnancy continued without any cause for concern.

Rachael and Billy went along to their twenty-week scan excitedly waiting to discover the sex of their baby. However, their worlds came crashing down when a serious genetic disorder called 'Patau syndrome' was discovered in the baby and the couple were told that their daughter was unlikely to survive the birth, and even if she did survive, she would live for no more than a few hours. Meanwhile, the levels of fluid building up inside Rachael were becoming dangerous and the couple were faced with the inevitability of terminating the pregnancy for medical reasons. 'I gave birth to my sleeping daughter Rose on 4 October 2013,' Rachael tells me.

The couple experienced the heartbreak and horror of a TFMR (a termination for medical reasons). I realise that I know absolutely nothing about this aspect of baby loss. How had I not come across this before? Of course I'm aware of baby loss and miscarriage, but I've never even heard of a TFMR, and I find that completely shocking. But I bet I'm not alone.

Following the TFMR, Rachael discovered the ARC charity, Antenatal Results and Choices, which specialises in helping parents and healthcare professionals through antenatal screening and its consequences.[10] ARC gave Rachael a great deal of help and support through her ordeal.

Before long, Rachael and Billy were expecting again. This time, Rachael's pregnancy ran through to full term and she gave birth to a healthy baby girl, Lucy, in October 2014. Throughout the various medical check-ups and scans during Rachael's second pregnancy, she happened across the same running midwife who had spoken to her before about her running experiences. This time around, Rachael listened more intently. She knew there was something important in this. She believed that running would become a part of their lives. In the following February, Rachael entered the ballot for the Great North Run. It was her intention to raise money for ARC, as they had helped her so much after the loss of her first daughter, Rose. This highlights the important role that charities play in helping people through times of deep personal crisis. When we talk about supporting people with their mental health, the role of charities often gets overlooked. Rachael's recovery from TFMR trauma was aided by the support she received from ARC. Often, the role of volunteers is fundamental in meeting the needs of people like Rachael, and many of those special individuals who volunteer their time do so because they have experienced the very same thing.

A few months passed and Rachael secured a place in the Great North Run. Billy gently reminded her that she hadn't yet run a single mile, and at the same time a health visitor informed her of a fitness scheme at the local leisure centre where there was a creche facility available if Rachael wanted to try out any of the fitness classes. 'I went along to a few of the classes and met some other people who were also running in the GNR,' she says. This was the turning point for Rachael, when the first threads of support gave her the impetus to take her challenge of running a half marathon seriously and to meet others who were on the same journey.

'I started to go out running by myself,' Rachael says. 'Billy asked me what trainers I was running in, and he couldn't believe it when I told him they were the same ones I had when I was a teenager!' Rachael invested in a new pair of running shoes and over the following months she began to make steady progress training towards her GNR goal. It wasn't pretty. She recalls having to phone Billy one day while out on a training run and asking him to collect her in the car. 'I'd run five miles and I honestly didn't think I could take another step,' she recalls. It reminds me of one of the races on my hotchpotch training schedule for my first London Marathon in 2011. It was a twenty-mile hilly route – further than I'd ever run before. I stopped on the brow of a hill at ten miles and rang home sobbing, pleading for a lift back home. When it became clear that wasn't an option, I continued to slowly put one foot in front of the other. I know how it feels to fully believe that you can't take another step forwards. Rachael did the same thing. She kept working slowly and steadily towards her goal. 'I don't know how, but I made it to the start line of the Great North Run,' Rachael says. She also made it across the finish line.

The journey to the Great North Run was a huge learning curve for Rachael. 'I'd been in a very bad place,' she says. 'I think it was more like post-traumatic stress disorder than postnatal depression.' She had been through a tumult of emotions in a very short time. From the devastation of her TFMR to the successful pregnancy and the accompanying cycle of hormonal changes, Rachael barely had time to step off the merry-go-round and pause for breath. However, while making her way steadily towards the goal of running the Great North Run, she had noticed how running was making her feel better. 'I slowly started to realise through my training that each time I went out running, I was feeling stronger and getting "the buzz".' The 'buzz' Rachael is referring to is of course the flood of endorphins brought on by physical exercise. Nature's very own antidepressant is so simple in its efficiency and effectiveness: all we need to do is step outside the front door to access it in abundance. Rachael pauses for a while and then says, 'I honestly think if I hadn't been running at that time, I would have turned to drinking.' We've heard this before, haven't we? Turning to alcohol to suppress and hide from our painful feelings is something that many people I've spoken to can relate to. That's not to say it's necessarily an 'either/or' choice, but running is certainly a healthier way of navigating those feelings for many of us when the alternative is so truly bleak.

After her first solo running journey and crossing the finish line of the Great North Run, Rachael metaphorically sat back down on the couch. Some time passed and Billy noticed how her mood had dropped. He understood the connection between running and Rachael's state of mind and suggested that she follow a Couch to 5k programme to get herself back into the habit of running again for her own mental wellbeing. This time, however, she wasn't alone on her running journey. A family friend was also doing the Couch to 5k, and so for the first time, Rachael began running regularly with others. This was a breakthrough. Although Rachael's solo journey to the Great North Run had given her a huge sense of personal achievement, it was by no means a running epiphany. Rachael found that running by herself didn't give her the motivation to keep going.

I love running alone, and much of my own running journey has been a solo effort, but Rachael didn't feel the same way. We're all different. But what came next would demonstrate the power of the running community to completely transform the lives of both Rachael and Billy. While progressing through the Couch to 5k programme, Rachael began to meet people and make friends. 'Me and my friend Donna started thinking about joining a local running club,' she tells me, 'but we were put off thinking that they were all "real runners" and we weren't.' I *so* know how she feels. This was me back in 2011 after I'd fumbled my way through the London Marathon and still felt like I wasn't 'one of them'. To make matters worse, Rachael and her friend decided to enter a local 10k race, not knowing that the running club used this as one of their target races. 'All the fast runners were there in their club vests,' she says. 'It was terrifying!' The two friends didn't come last, but they had been put off joining the running club. We've all been there. How was Rachael to know that this was a race chosen specifically because it was a fast, flat course, and that many of the running club members would have been training hard for months – if not years – to test themselves as part of a 'club handicap' competition? How were they to know that *not all* the runners in the club would be like whippets in vests tearing off at an alarming speed when the gun went off?

Weeks went by and eventually Rachael plucked up the courage to email her local running club. 'I knew I wanted to try it,' she says, 'it just took me a while to make that first contact.' Rachael received a lovely email in response, informing her of the club training nights and the times and places to meet. 'I sat on it for another few weeks before I finally took myself along,' she says. 'It felt like a huge thing for me to do.' And Rachael is right. It is a massive thing to turn up to a running club by yourself for the very first time. Recently, I've done the same thing with my local running club, and after years of running alone, it was terrifying sitting in my car watching people turn up and greet each other in their matching vests. And that is despite the fact that I have been a pretty serious runner myself for well over ten years!

Although that very first run with the club was nerve-racking, Rachael didn't regret her decision to be brave. Within just a few weeks she met one of her now best friends – another Rachael! 'We were at the same stage in our lives and had children of the same age,' Rachael tells me. 'We ran at a similar pace, and I began to look forward to our weekly running chats.' As Rachael kept going back to the club week after week, she began to meet more likeminded people and soon came to realise that they weren't the scary, intimidating bunch she had once feared. In fact, a year after she joined the running club, her husband, Billy, wanted in on the action. 'I think he saw this new part of my life and thought he may as well join in!' Rachael says. Billy began with the Couch to 5k programme. From there, he signed up to join the running club and before long he began to understand why it had been so transformative for Rachael. He began to make friendships of his own, and Rachael and Billy soon discovered a completely new social life. 'We've just come back from Edinburgh,' she tells me. A group from the running club go to run in the Edinburgh Marathon Festival each year, something Rachael and Billy are now very much a part of.

Rachael and Billy's story is inspiring because it is about a couple supporting each other along a completely new journey in life; one they never imagined taking. Yes, running helped Rachael to handle the devastation of the TFMR and the loss of her baby, Rose, but more than that, running became *a completely new life* for both Rachael and Billy in the years that followed. 'We were always known as a "fun-loving couple",' she tells me. We know what that means. These guys know how to party! But they began to discover how to have fun in a completely new way.

I have heard many stories of solo journeys throughout writing this book, but to hear of a couple who were more used to racing back to the bar than they were crossing finishing lines, and to discover how running opened up a whole new friendship group and social life for the pair who were hardly 'sporty types' is testament to the way that running can change lives in completely unpredictable ways. I'm sure that when Rachael and Billy met in 2011, they never imagined that they would become an integral part of the local running club and that their social worlds would expand beyond recognition. 'It's given us a new kind of social life,' Rachael says, while explaining that both she and Billy remain good friends with the people they were close to before their running epiphany – like getting the best of both worlds.

Running has also helped Rachael and Billy to curb their pre-running party lifestyle. 'I'll choose not to have that extra drink on a Friday night now if I've got a ten-mile run planned for the next morning!' Rachael tells me. It's all about moderation, isn't it? Not that I'm an authority figure on that myself, but it's certainly helped Rachael and Billy to have a happier, healthier and more balanced lifestyle. And they're doing it together. Isn't that a wonderful thing?

Since sharing her story with me, Rachael has recently completed the Montane Ullswater twenty-mile race with a friend. 'I'm not sure why I didn't think to look at the terrain or the elevation beforehand,' she says. For the next six and a half hours, the pair scrambled up mountains, across streams and down steep ravines in the blazing heat. 'We were overtaken by people with walking poles, pensioners and some who were dressed up as mountain goats.' Rachael dragged her friend to the finish after twenty-*three* miles. 'We staggered to the nearest pub and didn't move again for the rest of the night.' She isn't sure her friend will sign up to another race with her ever again!

Rachael has also run the London Marathon 2021 – eight years to the day since she went into hospital to give birth to her sleeping daughter, Rose.

# ANNA

I've spoken to people who have lost parents, husbands and children throughout the process of writing this book. All of them have been faced with a different kind of grief and they have learnt to deal with it in their own unique way. Of course, running plays a huge part in all the stories I have heard, but I have learnt that the process of coping with grief is a very personal thing. There is no 'one size fits all'.

Anna lives in Denmark. She contacted me when she heard that I was writing this book. Her message to me simply read:

> *Hi Rachel,*
> *I read that you were interested in hearing stories from people who have been helped by running. Running saved me when my sister died. Let me know if you want to hear more.*
> *Yours,*
> *Anna*

The loss of a sibling. This strikes me as being a particular kind of grief that I don't ordinarily hear very much about. I'm thinking of anybody I have ever met who has lost a brother or a sister, and I can only think of two people. The first is an old boss whose younger brother died in a tragic motorcycling accident in his twenties. It devastated his entire family, and my boss had found solace in his Christian faith in the years ever since. And then there's my dad. My dad's younger brother, David, died two decades ago, aged fifty-two. David went to play five-a-side football with his pals one evening and he suffered a heart attack from which he didn't recover. My uncle had two teenage girls at the time – just like my dad had two daughters, myself and my sister – and we were only a few years apart in age. I know that David's death had a profound impact on my dad, even though he has never talked to me about it very much. I know that he found it particularly difficult to deal with his younger brother's death because it didn't make any sense. How could his seemingly fit and healthy younger sibling just suddenly ... *die*? It wasn't just my dad's grief that consumed him; it was the sorrow of the family David had left behind: his wife and their two young daughters whose lives, at that moment, had been completely shattered.

Two decades later, my dad has a heart attack. Mercifully, it is only mild, but I can tell that it has shaken him to his core. He feels vulnerable; fragile even. My dad is a complex character. He's an easy-going kind of a chap but he's also a worrier, seemingly relaxed and chilled out on the surface, but underneath his jovial exterior there is a swell of anxiety that he has never wanted to acknowledge. Has he lived in fear of imminent death in the years ever since his younger brother died? Does he worry about a sudden pain in his chest and a tingling sensation down his arm? I believe that David's death changed something deep within my dad. I can only try to piece together what that is from my own observations and our conversations, and I realise that I will never know the true impact it has had on him.

Siblings. It's a deeply complex relationship spiked with emotions. With an older sister of my own, I wish I understood it more. It is from this perspective that Anna's story fascinates me. I wonder if I can gain any insight into my dad's thoughts and feelings. I try to place myself in Anna's shoes – thinking about my relationship with my own sister which I can't seem to fathom.

Anna's parents emigrated to Denmark from the UK before she was born. When Anna was just five years old, her parents returned to the UK, where they adopted Anna's younger sister, Margaret. Margaret was biracial. In the early 1970s, the family returned to live in Denmark, where Anna has remained ever since. Anna explains to me that at the time of their relocation, Denmark was not a culturally diverse country. Although she says that her ethnicity was certainly not the defining element of Margaret's life, it did mean that she stood out from the crowd. 'She was very visible,' Anna says. 'She was a larger-than-life character.'

The fact that her younger sister wasn't a blood relation will become relevant later in her story, but as young children, the two girls formed an extraordinarily close bond. Their sibling relationship continued to strengthen right through into adulthood.

We're galloping along at a pace and a lot happens in a very short time. I try to keep up with Anna as she is talking me through the chronology of events. It is exhausting just listening to her. Sadly, it appears that tragedy was all around.

Two years before Margaret became ill, her partner died by suicide. The shock of this reverberated throughout her entire life, and then in 2001 Margaret discovered that she had leukaemia. Leukaemia is a cancer of the blood, and it was necessary for Margaret to undergo stem-cell treatment. Efforts were made to trace Margaret's biological parents back in the UK but, sadly, they were not a match.

Within the space of just two years, Anna's sister Margaret had endured more tragedy than most people will know in an entire lifetime. Her partner had just died, and the manner of his death was particularly shocking. When a friend of mine died by suicide in 2005, the feelings of guilt and helplessness for not being able to do more were overwhelming. Plus, the sense of shock and horror felt like being pulled under water and not being able to come up for air. That was my friend. What must it be like for a partner – the person you love – to leave you in this way?

Tragically, Margaret even considered whether her cancer diagnosis was partly a result of the shock of her partner's suicide, wondering if the overwhelm and emotional onslaught of the whole experience literally broke her down. Anna tells me this without judgement. It is what her sister questioned about her own medical diagnosis, which would prove to be terminal. Even the fact that Margaret pondered this about her own illness speaks volumes about the depth of pain that she experienced when her partner died. To be so consumed with shock and grief that you consider it might have contributed to damage within your body tells you all you need to know about the impact of suicide by a loved one. And all the while, Margaret's sister, Anna, was right by her side as the waves of trauma, shock and devastation washed up not once but twice on Margaret's shores. How on earth must Anna have felt, to see her beloved sister living through this nightmare – or this series of nightmares – and to be utterly powerless to do anything about it?

During the four years of Margaret's intensive treatment for leukaemia, Anna lived very close to the hospital in which her sister was being treated. 'I used to go and see her in the hospital every day,' she says. 'We became incredibly close.' Sadly, Margaret finally succumbed to the illness, and she died in 2005. To help Anna manage the tsunami of pain, she decided to see a counsellor at this time. It sounds like a sensible thing to do. I can understand Anna putting on a brave face for her sister while she was going through years of cancer treatment and portraying an image of strength, positivity and resilience, which any of us would try to do if we were in her position. Perhaps Anna didn't want to show Margaret her sheer terror at the horrendous turn of events when it was her sister who was in hospital fighting for her life.

Once Margaret had died, the flood of sadness threatened to submerge Anna completely. 'I began to experience severe anxiety,' she tells me, despite never having been an anxious person prior to this episode. 'At one point, I was convinced that there was someone in our shower cubicle at home, and I became very anxious when travelling in cars.' Mental health illness affects everyone differently, and following the death of her sister, this was how it began to show itself in Anna's life. She also found it difficult to focus on her work. I'm fascinated by the body's myriad ways of managing stress and trauma. It can manifest in so many ways – ask anybody and their experience will be different to the next person's. To know that the seemingly bizarre feelings and inexplicable, intrusive thoughts such as those experienced by Anna are brought about by trauma is thought-provoking.

'In one of my counselling sessions, my therapist said to me, "Anna, either you start running or you will sink into a depression."' I have chosen to use the exact words as Anna has told them to me. Remember that this was fifteen years ago and the link between mental and physical wellbeing was not a conversation we were generally used to hearing. It may well be that Anna's therapist was way ahead of her time, and it's even more surprising that she made this particular suggestion, because Anna tells me that the woman wasn't a runner herself. I find it quite remarkable that a therapist in the mid-noughties suggested that one her clients should take up running as a *direct way* of mitigating the impact of her grief which might otherwise result in a mental health illness. It's not to say that running is by any means the only answer to grief or mental illness, but as part of the overall package of self-care it is certainly insightful. Who is this therapist? She deserves a medal.

It's clear that even after all this time, Anna still doesn't quite understand *why* this therapist had running in mind as a thing that could potentially be beneficial but – heeding the advice of the woman who was paid to help her manage her mental health – she decided to give it a go.

I ask Anna what she did from there and – you guessed it – we both laugh when she replies, 'I started running.' Yup. It was that simple. But how do you just begin to run from absolutely nowhere in the midst of overwhelming anxiety and grief? Did Anna set herself a goal or start following a training plan? Did she run by herself or seek out others to run with? There are so many ways of starting to run, I feel like mine wasn't such a daft question after all. Anna is a very straightforward person. She doesn't mess about. She tells me that quite simply she got a pair of trainers, and she … ran! 'I started to run on a treadmill at the gym,' she tells me. Interestingly, running on a treadmill was the thing that really worked for Anna at the time. She credits the routine of running on the treadmill three or four times a week with building a base level of fitness and confidence which meant that she then felt able to run anywhere – inside or out.

Treadmills get a lot of flak. People frequently moan about the boredom factor, and we've all heard the rather cutting reference to somebody having just been on the 'dreadmill'. Personally, I rather enjoy treadmill running. Like Anna, I have found that running on a treadmill has worked well for me at certain times in my life. I've run half marathon distances on a treadmill when the snow has piled up outside and I've executed speed work when time has been short – 5 x 5 minutes is a particularly harsh yet effective session for a lunchtime workout when you want to push the pace in a short amount of time. Anna adapted easily to treadmill running and she is one of the rare breeds like myself who doesn't find it a complete chore. She enjoys the fact that she can completely lose herself in her own thoughts on the treadmill. She likes the consistency of the pace and the fact that she can just 'zone out'. Now, don't get me wrong. I *love* running outside. There will be no contest there. But I also totally get that different people need different things from running at any given time, and for Anna, running indoors on a treadmill just *worked*! 'I started running for just ten or twelve minutes at a time,' she says, 'and I gradually built up to forty-five minutes, which was great because I could watch an entire episode of *Dr Phil* [her go-to show while treadmill running]'.

I ask Anna when she first began to feel the positive effects of running on her mental health in helping her come to terms with the loss of her sister. Interestingly, she says that she noticed how much better she felt once she began running outside. It sounds like the healing began to take place once Anna was running in nature. That's not to take anything away from the treadmill running which had built up Anna's fitness along with her confidence, but it is interesting how she seems to make the connection between running and the benefits for her mental health while she was running outside. She describes running outdoors as being 'meditative and healing', which are particularly strong therapeutic words for her to choose. Generally, however, Anna says that what she found most satisfying was setting goals – whether that was running indoors or out – and achieving them, feeling the progression and a sense of accomplishment which was applicable to both types of running. 'When things seemed utterly pointless, I found that even setting myself arbitrary goals was helpful,' she tells me. I understand what she means. On the face of it, the goal of 'running for twenty minutes on a treadmill' seems pretty futile, but for somebody who is feeling entirely consumed by helplessness without the ability to change anything, it can simply be a reason to keep moving forward and a sense of achievement on completion.

At the same time, Anna explains that she has a tendency to become obsessive over certain things, and at one point she felt this happening with running. To remedy this, Anna has set herself a monthly running limit of 100 kilometres. 'I've found that having this in place stops me from becoming too obsessed with my running goals, which can have a knock-on effect with other areas of my life,' she says.

I've never heard of this particular approach before. I've spoken to people who have chosen to work with a running coach to help them avoid this pitfall (myself and Kathryn included) but everybody is different, and if this works for Anna, then that's great! I admire Anna for not only being able to identify this in herself, but for putting things in place to avoid a scenario where running becomes a negative, destructive element in her life. She knows that if that happens, then she is more likely to become obsessive over other aspects, including – she tells me – food. This is a very dangerous, slippery slope and I can relate to it so strongly. It's remarkable how many people I've spoken to exhibit the same tendencies, and I certainly wish I'd been able to identify my predisposition to obsessive behaviour far earlier in my running journey. The message that running can help us is great, but we need to keep things in check, especially so for people like myself and Anna – and many others – who could so easily allow running to become an unhealthy obsession which turns a good thing sour. Nobody wants that, so being aware of this possibility is a vital part of any successful mental wellbeing tool kit. It sounds to me like Anna has got this spot-on. She gives me a knowing smile as we acknowledge our similarities with this side of our personalities.

I ask Anna what running has become to her since her sister died. Many years have passed, and I am interested to know how her running journey has developed. 'I love taking part in events,' Anna tells me. 'I don't consider them as races as such, but I love being a part of a collective running experience such as the Copenhagen Half Marathon.'

I would *love* to join Anna in running the event one year, and I've already earmarked it for my wish list when we can travel again. Anna selects a couple of running events to focus on each year, but the routine and regularity of running is far more important to her. 'When Covid hit, I increased my running from three times a week to running every other day,' she says. It was a subtle yet significant change in Anna's routine, upping her mileage to help her to cope mentally with the restrictions.

It seems as though Anna is extremely good at knowing instinctively what she needs to do to keep herself well. She is able to manage her running so that it has the maximum positive impact for her life without tipping over to an unhealthy place. I rather envy her levels of self-awareness and her instinct to know how to utilise running in the best possible way for herself. I finish our chat wishing that I'd had this conversation with Anna years ago. I realise that I could have learnt a lot from her then – as I have now.

Since sharing her story with me, Anna has continued enjoying running in her home city of Copenhagen. 'Because of the pandemic, there haven't been as many tourists where I live, so I have been able to run along the waterfront and through the old part of town which is normally packed out with people,' she says. 'I've seen the city in a whole new light, and it's been wonderful to see it gradually coming alive again following the pandemic.'

As for her future running goals, Anna tells me that she plans to run a marathon before she turns sixty. 'That's in three years' time, but I'm going to have to start running longer distances if I'm going to make that happen!'

# MARIA

My daughter, Tilly, is now eleven years old. For the past few weeks, we've been counting down to the summer holidays. It's funny how the six-week summer break feels like it will never arrive – counting down from four weeks … to three weeks … to two weeks … to one. This year I've been building myself up to deal with the fact that Tilly will be spending four weeks of the summer holiday – one whole calendar month – away from me. She will be staying with her dad and his family in the far north of Scotland. *For goodness' sake, Rachel. It's only four weeks!* the rational, logical voice inside my head reminds me. *Don't be so silly …*

Friday morning arrives – it's her last day of school. We rush through the usual pre-school-run checklist: 'Have you got your bag? Packed lunch? Your drink? Have you brushed your teeth?' She scurries around at the last minute, tripping over her own feet while collecting all her bits and pieces, as I stand by the open door shouting them out like a sergeant major – the last hour and a half having predictably been usurped by watching YouTube videos of cats and some indescribable nonsense on TikTok. Nothing new there. She isn't going to Scotland until tomorrow, but today, for some reason, it's hit me.

We set off in the car and I feel a bit choked up, but I manage to hold it together. Our usual Spotify playlist is on shuffle and Tilly is munching on her toast in the passenger seat, taking care to catch the crumbs in the paper towel which I insist she brings with her every day to prevent my car looking like a teenager's bedroom.

When she's finished her toast, I take hold of her hand between gear changes, and I notice how soft and warm her skin feels. Like the richest, purest silk. I could sit and stroke her hand for hours and marvel at how perfect it is. The playlist jumps to 'Here Comes the Sun'. *Oh no.* I can feel it coming. She's innocently singing along to the Beatles classic while I'm holding her perfect, silky hand, and it tips me over the edge. Silent tears are now streaming down my cheeks. How will I cope without her for four weeks? Will she be okay? Will *I* be okay? We spend every day of our lives – or certainly most days – together. We've survived many months of home-schooling, living in each other's pockets. Four weeks sounds like an eternity. How on earth will we cope without each other?

She looks over at me and smiles. 'It'll be okay, Mum,' she says, softly.

I laugh through my tears and say that I know it will. 'I just love you so much, Tills. That's all.'

I park up and she jumps out of the car, waving at me before skipping away, her long blonde hair swinging into the distance until she finally disappears through the school gates. I sit at the wheel of my car and sob uncontrollably. I know it's daft, but I'm a mum. I can't help it.

There's something universal about being a mum, isn't there?

I knew that of all of the stories I've listened to in the process of writing this book, Maria's would be the most difficult one for me to write. Ever since our conversation – the few hours that we spent talking over a Zoom call – I often replay parts of it in my head. This is the one that broke me. When I say that, what I mean is that I broke down during the call, which has never happened to me before or since. There is something so profoundly moving in speaking to a mother who has lost her daughter and has somehow managed to survive what is surely every mother's worst nightmare. I'm thinking about that car journey to school with Tilly and watching her mindlessly crunching on her toast; the feel of her soft, warm skin; her beautiful smile and the way she skipped off down the street. Maria has been robbed of all those tiny moments and many, many more. It takes every ounce of courage for me to even contemplate what that pain must be like, let alone consider how Maria has rebuilt her life since to be so full of joy *despite* the worst possible thing in the world happening to her: losing her little girl.

I need to prepare myself before putting on my headphones and replaying our conversation, and I take a moment to remind myself why it is so important for Maria to share her story. She wants others to know that survival from that place is possible. On the very day when I am about to begin writing her story, I receive a message from Maria. She tells me about a lady she knows whose two-year-old daughter has just died suddenly in the night. 'I sent her a card,' she says. 'I'm going to reach out to her in about a month or so – when things get real. I always pray that I can be of use to other mothers who join this awful club.' She tells me that this poor lady – the newest member of the worst club imaginable – is herself a runner. 'I'm going to share with her how slowly – very slowly – running saved me,' she says.

And so, I begin.

Before I start writing, I take another look at Maria's Instagram page. Posts pop up of her smiling selfies while she is out running on the trails and on the treadmill. To see that smile, you would never in a million years believe the horror that she has lived through; but that's the thing: she has not only somehow managed to survive it, but she has chosen to live the rest of her days joyfully and passionately and filled with purpose.

I take a deep breath and I press play. I can't help but notice that at the start of our call, I'm all smiles. I go through my usual pre-recording patter. Looking back on it now, I feel rather naïve – as though I hadn't anticipated the emotional tsunami which is about to hit me. I will be blown away by Maria's grace and her strength, and by her ability to talk to me so articulately about what must be one of the most inconceivably horrific experiences a person could ever endure.

This is Maria's story.

Maria is fifty-nine years old. She lives in Washington state with her husband, Tony. She has three grown-up children – a son and two daughters. She did have three daughters, but for over two decades she has had to learn to live without her youngest daughter, Jordan, who died at the age of five from a rare form of cancer.

Maria appears on my screen looking tanned, vibrant and much younger than her years. She is wearing a 'Boston running' skinny T-shirt. Her long, dark hair flows over her shoulders and her skin glows. For a moment I wonder what tragic story this woman might possibly have to share. She looks too ... *happy*! It lulls me into a false sense of security, and I begin our chat almost *disbelieving* that Maria has experienced any pain in her life at all, because *how on earth would she look like that if she had?* But we all make such judgements, don't we? We see a person who looks joyful and vibrant, and it simply doesn't make sense that they could be like that if they knew what real pain was. A tormented person would look different somehow, wouldn't they? They wouldn't be smiling, for starters. They might not bother to take care of themselves – possibly looking dishevelled and unkempt. A person who has experienced gut-wrenching, tormenting sadness would almost certainly *not* look like Maria does.

How utterly foolish I will soon feel.

Maria was born in a very small fishing village in Alaska on the small island of Kodiak. As a child she didn't have many opportunities to take part in sports, and because of this, she didn't have the confidence to try out for team sports at high school. 'So, I started running,' she says with a smile. 'Just on my own.' Maria ran throughout college – it was something she could do by herself. She tells me it helped her to manage her weight when the unhealthy habits of student life threatened to take their toll. 'I'd put on the typical college ten or fifteen pounds,' she says. I smile, knowing exactly what she means. Maria soon discovered that not only did running help her to look after her physical health, but it helped her to feel better mentally, too. 'Nobody talked about mental health or anxiety at the time,' she says, 'and I've struggled with anxiety throughout my life.'

Maria explains that she is by nature a perfectionist, an over-achiever and highly driven – she is somebody who places a lot of pressure on herself. Although it can be unhelpful to label people as having certain personality types, Maria says that she exhibits some of the classic characteristics of a person who is commonly inclined to suffer from mental health issues including depression and anxiety. This was certainly her experience, and she discovered that running helped her to manage this aspect of her personality.

Maria graduated from college and began her working life as a primary school teacher. 'I started running a few 5ks and 10ks ... like you,' she says, gesturing at the door behind me which is plastered in my old race numbers. She had children – three young daughters – and she started running again just as soon as she was able to after each of her girls was born. Maria's life was full. She was busy working as a teacher while bringing up her children. Life was good.

And then ...

Maria falls silent and looks upwards, as though she is accessing a place where there are many questions without any answers. 'You always think it happens to other people,' she says, as though all these years later she still can't believe that any of it happened.

Maria's daughter Jordan was just four years old.

Any parent will recognise the normality of their child being under the weather from time to time. We've all dealt with tummy bugs, and we've all had at least one call home from school with a child complaining of feeling poorly. There's nothing extraordinary about that, right? It happens to every parent at some time or another.

One day in January 1998, Maria received such a telephone call from Jordan's pre-school. They told her that Jordan was complaining of having a sore tummy and she 'just didn't seem quite right'. So, Maria did what any of us would do. She left work and she went to collect her young daughter. Typically, she wouldn't have called the GP for something as minor as a tummy ache, but she described having a 'sixth sense' that something else was going on. She telephoned and made an appointment for Jordan to see the GP, and – unusually – they told her to take Jordan in straight away. When Maria explained the situation to her principal (head teacher), she replied, 'I hope it's nothing serious', which Maria says in hindsight 'felt kind of odd'. All the tiny sixth-sense clues began to make Maria consider that this was perhaps something bigger than it first seemed.

But Jordan had a tummy ache. That's all ...

On examination, the paediatrician felt something unusual in Jordan's tummy and he sent Maria and her daughter off to the hospital for further tests. He offered a possible diagnosis of a kinked bowel, which isn't all that uncommon for a child to experience. 'I remember thinking on the way to the hospital, "Oh, I really hope it isn't a kinked bowel,"' Maria says, this being the worst-case scenario she could conceive of for Jordan at the time. 'In all the years since, I've desperately wished that it had been a kinked bowel.'

Jordan was in severe pain, clutching her tiny knees up to her chest. The usually vibrant, energetic, bubbly little girl was completely withdrawn. This made it impossible for the doctors to take an X-ray, but they did eventually manage to obtain an ultrasound image once Jordan had been sedated. 'They were all talking, lots of them in a huddle,' Maria says. 'I had no idea what was going on.' She tells me that a cancer diagnosis was so far removed from anything she could possibly imagine, 'They could have told me that we were flying to Mars tonight.' That would have had the same level of incredulity.

When the doctors finally told Maria that Jordan had cancer, she remembers feeling like she'd left her own body. 'It was surreal. I became completely separate from everything, as though I was floating above it all, watching what was happening beneath me.'

That night, Maria received more devastating news. Jordan's abdominal tumour was at stage 4 – the most advanced stage, meaning that it had spread to her lungs. She was also diagnosed with a rare heart condition *in addition to* her cancer diagnosis.

The facilities in their hometown – a small suburb in Alaska – were insufficient to deal with the magnitude of the medical emergency, so Maria and Jordan were immediately sent to a specialist children's hospital 1,400 miles away in Seattle.

Their lives would never be the same again.

Maria and Jordan now found themselves living in an oncology unit in a children's hospital in a city they didn't know. Their worlds had shifted not only towards the fear and devastation of Jordan's medical diagnoses, but towards uncertainty and change that they couldn't possibly comprehend. They were now living far away from family and friends – away from Maria's husband and her other two daughters. Maria was away from her job and her colleagues; Jordan was away from her two older sisters and her playmates. They had been teleported to the worst possible destination, and they would have to learn how to adapt and, if possible, how to survive. This was – as Maria describes it – quite literally a nightmare from which she couldn't wake up. The worst thing she could ever imagine *was now happening*. Take a moment to think about that. Imagine your entire life being turned upside down as the worst conceivable scenario unfolds right in front of your eyes. All from a tummy ache at school.

Maria describes how surreal everything around her had become. 'It was so noisy,' she says, explaining how suddenly being right in the epicentre of an oncology unit in a major children's hospital was a chaotic blur of beeping machines, painful cries and urgent, desperate voices. Imagine not only having to deal with your own shock and fear and that of your sick child, but having to listen to the wretched cries of other children and their families who were also living in their own personal nightmares. You can't block it out; you can't just up and leave when you've had enough and find a quiet, tranquil place far away from it all. You are stuck there with your critically ill child who is now on the ward for children with the most serious, life-threatening conditions on the planet.

It doesn't get any worse than that.

Maria is able to tell me about her experiences in such a measured, articulate way, I need to remind myself that she isn't telling me a story about another person's life. She has *lived through* this horror. This is *her life* we are talking about. It is *her daughter's life* which was hanging by a thread. It is *her entire support system* that she was now having to live without.

Jordan was placed into one of six individual critical care rooms which surrounded the 'command centre' (the nurses' station) in the middle of a semicircle. All the rooms had a glass window facing the command centre, where the various life-sustaining machines could be monitored around the clock. The sickest children in the entire hospital were located in each of the six rooms. Maria's daughter was one of them. Four words played on repeat in Maria's head: '*This can't be happening … This can't be happening … '*

But it *was* happening.

Humans are known for our resilience and our ability to adapt. We can survive in the most extreme places on the planet: from sulphur-caked desert plains to the vast and desolate fells of the Antarctic. Maria and Jordan had to adapt to survive on the high-dependency oncology ward of Seattle's Children's Hospital. 'It became our new normal,' Maria tells me. I don't know about you, but I would rather be forced to find ways to survive in *any other inhospitable corner of the planet* than there. I would rather be dropped into the middle of the Atacama Desert or given my marching orders to the remotest parts of Siberia than have to learn how to adapt – with my critically ill child – to living on a cancer ward in a children's hospital. But as we know, sometimes people don't get a choice. As the old adage goes, 'we are where we are'. And that's where Maria and Jordan found themselves.

Maria's husband had to return to work ... in Alaska. Their other two daughters had to continue to go to school ... in Alaska. So, Maria was left alone in Seattle with Jordan on a critical care cancer ward. Maria's teaching colleagues and friends rallied in support, raising funds to support Maria, who had to take time off work to be with Jordan, but – as she explains – the bills still needed paying and life continued to roll on despite the bomb which had just detonated in their lives. 'My other two daughters [aged eight and nine] didn't understand what was happening or why we couldn't go back home,' she tells me. 'They didn't know why their little sister had gone so suddenly, and why their mum had gone, too.' The impact of this unfolding horror show impacted on everyone. Nobody was spared.

Back at the hospital in Seattle, there was no difference between night and day. Maria describes it so vividly; I feel like I am right there. The hours merge into one another; the offensive, fluorescent lights are the same around the clock. The machines don't stop making noises at night-time: they are likely to be keeping a critically ill child alive, after all. 'Sleep was non-existent,' Maria tells me. Even in the most tranquil setting imaginable with flickering candles and soothing music, how impossible would it be to sleep knowing that your child's life was in peril? I struggled to sleep for a week when Tilly fell off a wall and smashed up her face. She didn't even break her nose or lose any teeth, and I still woke up in a cold sweat wondering whether she would be scarred for life and when the visible grazes would heal. This? This is a different level altogether. In my mind, this is never having another peaceful night's sleep again.

Maria was offered accommodation in the hospital's Ronald McDonald House – a charity set up to support families like Maria's who are forced to stay away from home while their sick children undergo intensive long-term medical treatment. However, with Jordan undergoing chemotherapy at levels so high that they would have almost certainly killed an adult (children are able to tolerate higher doses because of their rapid cell growth), it was impossible for Maria to leave her bedside. Instead, she kept vigil over her daughter and slept in 'The Blue Chair' beside Jordan's bed for – and I still can't quite comprehend this – eight months.

The Blue Chair became Maria's new home. It was where she spent twenty-four out of every twenty-four hours. I've seen a photograph of her sitting in The Blue Chair with Jordan on her lap, fast asleep with tubes and wires hooking her up to various machines. To think that this is where Maria *slept* – if she slept at all – is just mindboggling. Have you ever fallen asleep in a lounge chair? Perhaps you dozed off during a film and woke up with a start, wondering why you ached everywhere. This was Maria's *LIFE*. Quite simply, Jordan was so incredibly poorly that Maria never got to spend a single night in a bed at the Ronald McDonald House. She couldn't leave her side. So, she spent night after endless, wretched night in The Blue Chair.

January turned to February, which bled into March and drifted into April. 'The nurses had come to know me very well,' Maria says. 'There was one particular nurse who I became incredibly close to.' Kristy was Jordan's favourite nurse, and she knew that Maria was a runner. One day, Kristy took Maria aside. 'You know,' she said gently, 'you really need to start getting out of this hospital. Even if it's only for half an hour.' Kristy saw that Maria's twenty-four-hour bedside vigil was taking its toll. Kindly and gently, she suggested that it might be time for her to consider taking a step outside the hospital. Away from The Blue Chair; away from Jordan. This was a big deal. This was a *huge* deal for Maria to even contemplate. Leaving her daughter's bedside had – up to this point – been inconceivable. *What if something happens while I'm away? What if she needs me? What if … the unthinkable happens?* Kristy had grown very close to Jordan and Maria, and it was only from this firm base of trust and love that she felt able to make such a suggestion.

For the first time during our call, Maria becomes teary-eyed, at the memory of Kristy suggesting that she take a break for just *half an hour* out of every day.

That's it. I'm gone. I can't speak. And there's no point in me even pretending to get a handle on it, either. Maria comes in to help me. 'It's okay,' she says. 'I get it. When you're a mum, it's kinda hard, isn't it?' I nod pathetically. I still can't form any words. 'No one can understand the love you have for your child, right?' she says, trying to comfort me – a mother who only a matter of days ago was sobbing at the prospect of being separated from my daughter for just *four weeks*. I don't know where to look. Maria tells me that the other mothers she has since met who have also lost children call it being 'in the club'. She explains that just as it is impossible to wrap words around the depth of love a mother has for her child, so the feelings of pain and loss of those who are 'in the club' are also indescribable.

I'm in bits. Snot and tears are streaking down my face and Maria is comforting *me*! Thinking about it now, I guess it's shocking to hear a story like Maria's in her own words. We read about horrible things happening in the media all the time, but to talk to a person and for them to tell you about living through an experience like this is on another level completely. Hearing some terrible, tragic story via a third party is still awful, but it separates 'us' from 'them'. It keeps tragedy a safe distance away from us. This is completely different. My emotions are raw; I feel exposed. There is nowhere to hide, and I can't simply look away. Just as Maria said in the first few minutes of our chat, 'You always think it happens to other people.' Never has anything or anyone managed to dispel that myth for me more than Maria has done. This stuff *does* happen. It happens every day. It happens all over the world to lovely, honest-to-goodness people just like you, me and Maria.

But this isn't just a story about tragedy. It is a story about hope and resilience. It is a story about survival and recovery from the most seemingly impossible place.

Kristy – the angel nurse who whispered gentle words of concern into Maria's ear – may not have been aware of their significance at the time. She said, 'You need to call home and ask for your running shoes to be sent over.'

This was the moment, a pivotal moment when Maria was forced to confront the reality that she had a duty to take care of *herself* – even for thirty minutes in a day – despite the care that she still needed to give to her critically ill daughter around the clock. It wasn't something she'd even considered before Kristy quietly reminded her that it was okay to do that. Kristy was brave. She voiced what Maria already knew deep inside. She knew that ultimately, she would need to begin to take care of herself again. She needed to be strong for Jordan and for the rest of her family; she needed to be mentally well enough to endure whatever was around the corner, which, of course, nobody yet knew.

When Maria finally did get hold of her trainers, she made herself go out running – just for half an hour at a time. 'It was really hard,' she says. 'The guilt was real. And the panic.'

Following months of a twenty-four-hour bedside vigil, Maria finally took the opportunity to allow herself a chink of daylight in an otherwise institutionalised existence, all thanks to her angel nurse. 'Kristy was the only person I would trust to stay with Jordan whilst I was out running,' Maria tells me. Can you imagine that level of trust? What would it take for you to leave the bedside of your critically ill child for a thirty-minute reprieve with those four words on endless repeat: *WHAT IF SOMETHING HAPPENS?* Let's take a moment to remember that this was a time when very few people had mobile phones. There wasn't the option for Kristy to call Maria should something unthinkable happen to Jordan while she was out running. For those thirty minutes, Maria was completely unreachable while Jordan was critically ill in hospital, in somebody else's care.

'I was literally untethered from her for that thirty-minute window,' Maria says. 'It was so tough to be able to do that, and I couldn't have even considered it without Kristy. The nurses like Kristy not only nurse the children in their care, but also their families,' she says.

Maria is right. These people are angels right here on earth. They spend their lives caring for the sickest children and the most devastated parents at the worst possible time of their lives. Kristy wasn't just a nurse to Jordan; she was also a life support to Maria.

Maria began to go out running for thirty minutes a couple of times a week, and before long she began to notice the way it helped her to process all of the emotions that were trapped inside. 'I would cry when I ran,' she says, 'because I couldn't let myself cry in front of Jordan.' Like a lid coming off a pressure cooker, running allowed Maria to finally begin to process all the worries, fears and trauma she was now living. The strong, resilient, fearless mum could at last allow her protective walls to come down for a short while and allow herself the freedom to escape temporarily from everything happening around her. 'Some days I would cry; other days I wouldn't. It became a place where I could allow my body and mind to do whatever they needed.'

Maria describes these runs as being 'restoring' – as though they gave her just enough time, space, release and rejuvenation for her to return to her daughter and her role as a strong, resilient, fearless mother once again. 'It got the pain out; it got the fear out, and – oh, my God – just GETTING OUTSIDE!' From spending twenty-four hours a day surrounded by the sight, sound and smell of machines and desperately sick children, getting outside for a run was like drowning and then coming up for air. Maria soon discovered the Burke–Gilman Trail – a converted old railway line which weaves its way through Seattle. 'The Pacific Northwest is just gorgeous,' she tells me, her face beaming.

Meanwhile, Jordan's cancer treatment was going well. The primary tumour had shrunk to the size of a walnut and the secondary cancers had seemingly disappeared. Preparations were then made to rectify the problem with her heart, and surgery was planned. As the date for the heart operation approached, a final CT scan was arranged to make sure that the cancer treatment was still on track so that the heart surgery could take place. Imagine the pressure of balancing two life-threatening conditions of a four-year-old little girl. As if one of those wasn't enough. I could go on to kick and scream and eulogise about 'fairness', asking unanswerable questions about WHY THESE THINGS HAPPEN, but what's the point? They just do.

The CT scan was carried out in the August. Jordan and Maria were by then in their *tenth month* of this ongoing nightmare. But when the results of the scan came back, the doctor told Maria that he wanted to wait until the social worker was present to talk to her about the results. Oh my God. Yes, I know what you're thinking. I'm thinking the same. Maria was also convinced that this indicated a certain outcome – the most likely one being that Jordan's cancer had returned. 'As soon as they mentioned the social worker, I just knew,' she says. 'It's like the angel of death. That's just what happens.' Her husband disagreed, trying to rationally consider the infinitely more hopeful possibilities. But sometimes a gut feeling is there for a reason. Sometimes we just know things – sometimes inconceivably awful things – and we get advanced warning that they are coming our way.

Maria was right. Jordan's cancer had returned. Once again, she had the out-of-body experience; once again she was floating above it all, watching the conversations happening beneath her. Her next words make me cry again. 'How long?' she asked. She was asking how much longer her four-year-old daughter had got left to live. Imagine that. A death sentence for your daughter has now been confirmed – you just don't know the date yet.

As often happens in such cases, the next stop is home. It was a small mercy for Jordan to at least be able to live out her final days in the comfort of the place she called her home. Away from the life-supporting machines and the overwhelming stench of critical care.

Jordan returned home on the Saturday. She died a week later.

'I just wanted to lie down and not get back up,' Maria says. The weight of the grief was too heavy to bear. But she had two other daughters to take care of. There was no choice. She *had to* get back up.

Maria couldn't return to work. Turning up to teach schoolchildren who were the same age as Jordan every day was simply too much to ask.

It's August 1998. Maria's youngest daughter has just died; she is now living back at home with her husband and their two children. She is functioning, but only just. And rather like the nurse Kristy who saved her before, Maria was about to encounter another angel. One day, a good friend said to her, 'Why don't you put your running shoes on whilst the girls are at school?' Maria knew that if she didn't, if she crawled back into her bed and pulled over the covers, there was every chance that she would never come back out again. It felt like another crossroads. She would have to make a choice: to either put her running shoes back on, or to crawl away and allow her sadness to consume her entirely. Maria truly believed that her heart was so completely broken, she tells me: 'I thought to myself: "I could die from this."'

We know what she chose to do.

She put on her running shoes.

'At first, I cried every time I ran,' she says. 'But then very slowly, it got better.'

Read those two lines again, slowly this time. *SHE PUT ON HER RUNNING SHOES ... AND VERY SLOWLY, IT GOT BETTER.* If you ever wanted to see first-hand the power of running and its ability to heal, then these two lines do it for me. Maria had lost her daughter. She almost died inside from the weight of that pain. And running helped her – not only during the many months when she held a twenty-four-hour vigil at her daughter's bedside, but once she was gone. Running helped Maria at the worst moments in her life, during the worst experience imaginable.

Maria is a person who needs to have order in her life. She has specific ways of doing things. She is meticulous – sometimes to the point of obsession. We chat about it and conclude that we both share this trait; we think it could be something to do with having a need to control something – anything – in a world where ultimately, we realise that we don't have very much control at all. 'When your child gets sick and dies, your whole world is out of control,' Maria says. 'You can't control ANYTHING. You can't control what is happening to your child, and you can't fix it.'

So, when Maria started running again after Jordan had died, she could finally control *something*. It makes perfect sense to me. 'I could set myself goals; I could structure my training; I could choose my distance and my run route; I could work out a plan for my week. All of it was within my control.'

Soon, Maria was keeping a run diary and her mind was completely focused on running – a welcome reprieve from soul-crushing grief. 'It made it possible for me to get out of bed when, quite honestly, I just wanted to crawl back into it once the girls were at school.' Running every day enabled Maria to survive. She could get up, get dressed and put tea on the table when her two daughters returned home from school each day.

The epiphany didn't happen overnight – she tells me that most days she ran instinctively, without thinking, as though it was a primal survival mechanism. It was only after months of doing this that she realised the profound effect running had on her life. 'Running became like having a spiritual experience every day,' she says.

The following May, Maria and her two daughters ran the annual Anchorage Heart 10k race together – an event to raise funds for the local cardiac unit and raise awareness of cardiac disease. The next day, there was a huge photograph of Maria and her daughters in the local newspaper, and their story of running for Jordan. 'It was our way of keeping her memory alive,' Maria says. She went on to take part in other running events, explaining that 'it helped to keep me out of the black hole'.

Maria went on to have a little boy a year and a half after Jordan died, and she believes that running has enabled her to live her life being able to deal not only with the devastation of losing Jordan, but with her pre-existing mental health challenges. 'Running has helped me to manage my anxiety and to slow down the hamster wheel of my runaway, unhelpful thoughts,' she tells me. Maria had discovered the many healing properties of running before her world fell apart, and then she was guided right back to it at the times when she needed it the most. She has learnt through her experience that running is a part of recovery. 'It can help a person recover from the worst imaginable things.'

Fast-forward to the present day. Maria's job means that – pre-Covid – she was required to travel all across the US. It's a part of her work that she has also managed to adapt into her running life. She tells me about the running routes she has discovered in Louisiana, Washington and Florida … and any number of other US states. 'Running helps me with jet lag and tiredness and it helps me to familiarise myself with the new places I go to,' she says. It even helps her to connect socially with her clients, as she often opens up conversations by asking, 'Where should I go running around here?'

So, as a natural progression from her jet-setting across the US and running wherever she landed, Maria decided to set herself the challenge to run fifty races in fifty states in her fifties. At the time Covid hit, she was almost halfway to realising her goal, but then – as we know – life happens, and things take an unexpected turn. Maria smiles as she says, 'I know I won't complete all fifty races whilst I'm in my fifties, but I'll keep going anyway!'

I ask Maria what her proudest running achievement has been. 'The year I turned fifty, I ran the Maui Marathon in Hawaii,' she says. 'What I discovered was that training for and running a marathon is a lot like grieving. It's not something that happens overnight and it's not necessarily linear progress.' Maria describes how she found running a marathon to be painful, and the progress to reach that point takes time. 'Whilst there is measurable progress, there are also the bad days and setbacks that come along as part of the journey. There are days when you doubt you can do it and feel like quitting, and others when you feel more hopeful and start to believe that you might just be able to do this seemingly impossible thing after all. And in the end, you are surprised at what you're capable of with time, hard work and the support of those that love you. Just like grieving.'

The Maui Marathon holds a particularly special place in Maria's heart. 'A friend of mine who lives in New York City flew out to Hawaii to support me during the race,' she tells me. 'The morning of the race, my husband, son and daughters helped me load up the SUV ready to drive to the start. My friend, Elizabeth, showed up with a bike which she had rented so that she could ride to certain points on the course and check on my progress.' Maria talks about her pre-race anxiety and feeling an enormous sense of fear over letting everyone down, her mind tail-spinning into worst-case-scenario outcomes. One question in particular tormented her: 'What if I can't finish?' Well, she did finish. 'When I crossed the finish line, I sobbed with joy, relief, and gratitude for what running has done to make my life better in so many ways.'

I love Maria's attitude. I love the fact that for so many years, her love for running wasn't driven by her ego or pursuing outcomes. It came from a place that is so primal and so deep within all of us – it came from an innate knowledge about how to survive. Even when rational thought had no place – when she was too broken and mentally exhausted to think – she *still* knew instinctively to put on her running shoes.

Maria's evolving relationship with running over the last two decades is a truly wonderful thing. They have grown together; they have travelled together. They have been through fear and grief and overwhelming sadness together, but also through joy and celebration and triumph together. Running has played so many support roles in Maria's life, it is impossible to pinpoint one over another. I think that perhaps we can all take something from this. We can all learn to love and appreciate running, however it manifests, at whatever time in our lives.

Months have passed. I often replay parts of my conversation with Maria in my head. It's difficult to put into words how her story has impacted on me. Perhaps it's because I'm a mum to my own little girl; perhaps it's because hearing about Maria's experience in her own words made it feel so much closer to home. But I think that Maria's story affected me so deeply because of her ability to live a joyful life following Jordan's death. Maria's joy for running is contagious. She oozes passion and gratitude and a deep love for the thing which has been so pivotal in her life for such a long time. This is no longer a story about trauma and tragedy. It is a celebration of being truly alive.

Since sharing her story with me, Maria has taken on a new job as a school principal. 'For the first time ever, I'm trying to figure out how to balance work and life,' she says. 'I know that if I put running on the back-burner, I won't be able to cope with the stress of this new job. I believe I would also risk falling into some kind of depression.' Despite this enormous change to Maria's lifestyle, she is committed to picking up on her 'fifty races in fifty states' goal. 'Sure, I'll have to adapt it a little, as I'm now fifty-nine,' she says, 'but I hope to run several races this spring and summer to check off at least four to six more US states.'

And finally, she says this: 'Running is a part of my life that I love, and I am grateful for every single day. Running has taught me so many lessons, most of all that I am stronger than I think, and that I can survive the most horrible thing that anyone can ever imagine – the death of my child. Running has saved my life.'

I have no words other than these: Maria, you are my hero. And I salute you.

# LEARNING LESSONS

Over the past two decades, running has taught me a great deal about myself and about life. It dawned on me that running isn't the only tool for learning. It has long since been my belief that we can learn from hearing *each other's* stories. That was my purpose in writing this book. We can take comfort in our shared experiences and we can begin to understand ourselves better as a result.

Throughout the process of writing this book I have been submerged in a learning journey. Whilst listening to the incredible stories that you have just read and meeting the people who have contributed to this book, I realised that from each and every one of them I have learnt something different, something unique. I'm sure you will have your own lasting impressions. You will relate to the stories in ways that I do not, and that is a wonderful thing. We take what we need from each other, and in the echo chamber of our common life experiences, there will always be differences. It delights me to now think of all these people as my friends. However our paths have crossed, these are people that I can relate to on many levels. I've had the great fortune to speak to them personally and to spend some time learning about their lives. These are the things that I have taken from each of their stories.

From Carly I've learnt that it is possible to see past my physical imperfections and to focus on what my body can do.

From Martin I've learnt that it is possible to start running at any age and to get really good at it!

From Lisa I've learnt the power in sharing a running goal and the collective healing that can bring.

From Gina I've learnt that it's possible to completely redesign your life from the building blocks of running.

From Lars-Christian I've learnt about running with purpose, and the strength of making a commitment to yourself.

From Hannah I've learnt that chronic pain is truly debilitating and that running can open incredible doors for recovery.

From Felicity I've learnt that running can expand the life of a person who finds themselves socially isolated and alone.

From Judi I've learnt that creating a whole new life is possible when you're brave and take risks – like strapping yourself to a couple of dogs as they fly down trails!

From James I've learnt that sometimes you just need to complete a journey in life – running or otherwise.

From Liz I've learnt that I have a running twin! I've learnt that running can be a vent at the hardest times and can be a way of letting go of fear and frustration.

From David I've learnt that my history of bipolar disorder might go some way to explaining my irrational and excessive tendencies towards overtraining.

From Helen I've learnt that running can be a double-edged sword. It can heal and it can hurt you. Treat with caution.

From Kathryn I've learnt that it is possible to move beyond your own shame and focus on positive motivations, instead.

From Rachael I've learnt that running can heal and transform a couple's lives, paving the way for a healthier and a happier future together.

From Anna I've learnt that running can appear in your life out of nowhere, and before you know it, you can't imagine what you would do without it.

From Maria I've learnt that it is possible to overcome the worst kind of pain, the loss of a child. I've learnt that it is possible to survive and to live a joyful and purposeful life.

The people I've met in the process of writing this book are a huge source of inspiration to me. At a time when I have faced my own (admittedly very modest) challenges, they symbolise strength and determination, and every single one of them has taught me something about overcoming adversity and the deep well of strength and resilience that is a part of the unbreakable human spirit.

I have also learnt to be kind to myself. I've learnt that as much as running has played a huge part in my own journey and my recovery from mental health illness, it doesn't define me. I've learnt that my self-worth has finally taken root in far more solid ground than that.

I've learnt that I am not defined by running or by my personal best times, and I have learnt to enjoy the journey – even the bumpy parts – instead of just waiting for the end destination to arrive.

I've learnt to let go of my ego and to submerge myself in the stories and the strength of others, and in that way, I can begin to rebuild my own.

# ACKNOWLEDGEMENTS

**When you believe in something so strongly and you lean into that belief, incredible things happen.**

I was fully committed to writing a book about other people's stories and how running has helped them at pivotal times in their lives. I didn't know how it would happen; I just knew if I followed my instinct and kept taking tiny steps forward, that it would.

What happened next was incredible. From the support of Saucony UK to the belief in this project from my literary agent, Jo Bell, it started to build in momentum. And then the real magic happened …

I met the incredible people whose stories I would share. Somehow, they happened across my path. I've been lucky enough to listen to and write their stories, and my heart is completely full of the love I've received from those people with whom I now share a special bond.

It has been one of the hardest and the best experiences of my life to listen to their words and to feel their pain – and their joy – at overcoming some of the hardest challenges of being human. To all those who have contributed to the stories within this book, you are all brave and bold and I have made some lovely and special friends along this journey. My biggest thanks go to you.

In addition, this project wouldn't have been possible without the support of Gareth Lloyd at Saucony UK and Nick Anderson at Running With Us who saw the value in sharing everyday stories of runners just like me, many of whom had reached out to me after I'd shared my own journey in the pages of a book.

I am also sincerely grateful for the support and encouragement from others in the very early days of conceptualising this book, including Jaimie Fuller, Jim Miles (Brooks) and Lucy Johnson (Polar UK), who have each, in their own way, contributed to the swell of belief that writing this book might be possible.

Thanks to my mum for proofreading *yet another* A4 binder filled with pages I have written, and to my dad for not making any mention of either running or writing, and instead focusing on how well I can bake bread and/or a cake. Thanks to my lovely friend Rhiannon for our many walks and talks and for helping to clear my head when it has felt to be bursting at times, and to Jules who has done the same (we met up again after twenty-five years directly because of me writing this book).

Thanks to the team at Vertebrate who took me and this project under their wing and who have indulged me in joining their list of esteemed authors, all of whom I respect enormously. Thanks also to Jon and Kirsty for taking me on a run from the Vertebrate office and crediting me with having a 'graceful running style'. That means more to me than you will ever know.

While this book has taken up most of my conscious thoughts and waking hours over the past twelve months, I have been supported every single day by the two people who know more about what that journey has been like than anyone else: my husband, John, and my daughter, Tilly. John, thank you for making my lunches every day and for the date walks into town. Tilly, thanks for letting me take my Zoom calls in peace and not invading the office bedroom with ukulele playing, as unquestionably talented as you are.

Ultimately, this book is my way of thanking a small group of particularly brave individuals for helping the rest of us learn how to heal.

# NOTES

1 Quoted in www.cancercenter.com/cancer-types/breast-cancer/stages

2 Data taken from the Office for National Statistics coronavirus roundup on 3 November 2020, at which point 49,420 out of 55,311 deaths registered in England and Wales had mentioned 'Covid-19' on the death certificates: www.ons.gov.uk/peoplepopulationand-community/healthandsocialcare/conditionsanddiseases/articles/coronaviruscovid19roundupdeathsandhealth/2020-06-26

3 Jürgen Barth, Sarah Schneider & Roland von Känel (2010), 'Lack of social support in the etiology and the prognosis of coronary heart disease: a systematic review and meta-analysis', *Psychosomatic Medicine*, 72(3), 229–238. https://doi.org/10.1097/PSY.0b013e3181d01611

4 Aparna Shankar, Mark Hamer, Anne McMunn & Andrew Steptoe (2013), 'Social isolation and loneliness: relationships with cognitive function during 4 years of follow-up in the English Longitudinal Study of Ageing, *Psychosomatic Medicine*, 75(2), 161–170. https://doi.org/10.1097/PSY.0b013e31827f09cd

5 Lisa M. Jarenka, Christopher P. Fagundes, Ronald Glaser, Jeanette M. Bennett, William B. Malarkey & Janice K. Kiecolt-Glaser (2013), 'Loneliness predicts pain, depression, and fatigue: Understanding the role of immune dysregulation', *Psychoneuroendocrinology*, 38(8), 1310–1317. https://www.sciencedirect.com/science/article/abs/pii/S0306453012004039?via%3Dihub

6  Louise C. Hawkley, Ronald A. Thisted, Christopher M. Masi & John T. Cacioppo (2010), 'Loneliness predicts increased blood pressure: 5-year cross-lagged analyses in middle-aged and older adults', *Psychology and Aging*, 25(1), 132–141. https://doi.org/10.1037/a0017805

7  John T. Cacioppo, Mary Elizabeth Hughes, Linda J. Waite, Louise C. Hawkley & Ronald A. Thisted (2006), 'Loneliness as a specific risk factor for depressive symptoms: cross-sectional and longitudinal analyses', *Psychology and Aging*, 21(1), 140–151. https://doi.org/10.1037/0882-7974.21.1.140

8  Julianne Holt-Lunstad, Timothy B. Smith, Mark Baker, Tyler Harris & David Stephenson (2015), 'Loneliness and social isolation as risk factors for mortality: a meta-analytic review', *Perspectives on Psychological Science*, 10(2), 227–237. https://doi.org/10.1177/1745691614568352

9  www.worldobesity.org/news/statement-coronavirus-covid-19-obesity

10 www.arc-uk.org/about-arc/

# HELPFUL RESOURCES

Being mindful that running is by no means the only thing that helps people in times of distress and adversity, we asked all our contributors for their personal recommendations of other helpful resources. The collection below is by no means exhaustive, and many of our contributors have received the benefit of personal counselling and/or therapy of one kind or another. However, we wanted to share these other resources that have helped them in various ways.

## CHARITIES AND SUPPORT

- Antenatal Results and Choices (*www.arc-uk.org*) – charity offering support and advice to parents who receive a bad diagnosis in pregnancy. ARC also have a forum for parents to chat in a safe place.
- BDD Foundation (*www.bddfoundation.org*) – Body Dysmorphic Disorder Foundation
- Beat (*www.beateatingdisorders.org.uk*) – support for people with eating disorders
- Forward Leeds (*www.forwardleeds.co.uk*) – the drug and alcohol service in Leeds
- Smart Recovery (*www.smartrecovery.org.uk*) – helping people recover from addictive behaviour
- The 401 Foundation (*www.facebook.com/the401foundation*) – Ben Smith, who ran 401 marathons in 401 days, set up this foundation to help local communities empower individuals to build confidence and self-esteem

- The Daisy Network (*www.daisynetwork.org*) – charity for anyone affected by POI (premature ovarian insufficiency)/early menopause

## WEBSITES AND SOCIAL MEDIA

- CaniCross (*www.canicross.org.uk*) – all about trail running with dogs
- James Clear (*www.jamesclear.com*) – writing about habits, decision making and continuous improvement
- @menagainstmountains on Instagram – very honest, quite gritty account with an incredibly supportive little community around it
- Parkrun UK (*www.parkrun.org.uk*) – information about the free weekly events
- The Single Supplement (newsletter *https://thesinglesupplement.substack.com* or Facebook group *www.facebook.com/groups/544538106156074*) – friendly and supportive community for those forging a life as single people
- Victorian Nursery (*www.victoriananursery.co.uk*) – fantastic independent nursery for sourcing interesting seeds and plants; just opening the box in the mail will put a smile on your face
- Yoga with Adriene, available on YouTube (*www.youtube.com/c/yogawithadriene/videos*) – and yoga in general; yin yoga for getting at the deep tissues is especially good

## PODCASTS

- Happy Place – Fearne Cotton talks to people about what happiness means to them
- Her Spirit – Louise Minchin and Annie Emmerson talk to strong, inspirational women
- Running Commentary – comedians Paul Tonkinson and Rob Deering talk about life and running
- Tell Me About Your Pain – Alan Gordon and Alon Ziv talk about relieving chronic pain
- Terrible, Thanks for Asking – young widow Nora McInerney talks to people who have had terrible experiences

## APPS

- Calm – help with sleep, mediation and relaxation
- Couch to 5k – running plan for beginners and people who want to get more active
- Fiit – fitness app with classes to help with mental health, mood and sleep, including yoga classes with Richie Bostock (see also *www.thebreathguy.com*) and breathwork classes with Richie Norton (see also *www.thestrengthtemple.com*)
- Headspace – meditation and mindfulness to reduce stress

## BOOKS

- *26.2 Miles to Happiness: A comedian's tale of running, red wine and redemption* by Paul Tonkinson
- *Running for My Life* by Rachel Ann Cullen
- *Running Free: A runner's journey back to nature* by Richard Askwith
- *Self-Help for Your Nerves: Learn to relax and enjoy life again by overcoming stress and fear* by Dr Claire Weekes
- *The Gift: 12 lessons to save your life* by Edith Eger
- *The Runner: Four years living and running in the wilderness* by Markus Torgeby
- *The Unexpected Joy of Being Sober* by Catherine Gray
- *Uncoupling: How to survive and thrive after breakup and divorce* by Sara Davison
- *Untamed: Stop pleasing, start living* by Glennon Doyle
- Other recommended authors for health and wellbeing include Poorna Bell, Matt Haig, Kris Hallenga, Bella Mackie, Fearne Cotton, Adriene Herbert and Bryony Gordon.